Hjalmar Hjorth Boyesen

Literary And Social Silhouettes

Hjalmar Hjorth Boyesen
Literary And Social Silhouettes
ISBN/EAN: 9783744651752
Printed in Europe, USA, Canada, Australia, Japan
Cover: Foto ©ninafisch / pixelio.de

More available books at **www.hansebooks.com**

BY

HJALMAR HJORTH BOYESEN

NEW YORK
HARPER AND BROTHERS
MDCCCXCIV

Copyright, 1894, by HARPER & BROTHERS.

All rights reserved.

CONTENTS

	PAGE
TYPES OF AMERICAN WOMEN	1
GERMAN AND AMERICAN WOMEN	24
THE AMERICAN NOVELIST AND HIS PUBLIC	41
THE PROGRESSIVE REALISM OF AMERICAN FICTION	58
THE HERO IN FICTION	79
AMERICAN LITERARY CRITICISM	97
AMERICA IN EUROPEAN LITERATURE	117
THE ETHICS OF ROBERT BROWNING	131
MARS vs. APOLLO	147
PHILISTINISM	163
SOME STRAY NOTES ON ALPHONSE DAUDET	178
MY LOST SELF	194
THE MERIDIAN OF LIFE	205

TYPES OF AMERICAN WOMEN

ERBERT SPENCER insinuates in one of his sociological works that the indirection, the coquetry, the *finesse*, nay, all the arts which we find so adorable in women, are modified forms of hypocrisy. Before the advent of civilization, woman had in pure self-defence to practise an elaborate deception. In order to please her brutal lord and secure predominance among dangerous rivals, she had to disguise her natural sentiments, and return caresses for blows and smiles for discourtesy. As she could not accomplish her purposes by force, she became an expert in domestic diplomacy. The craftier, the more guileful, she was, the better were her chances of survival. And thus it has come to pass that, though the necessity for intricate behavior is now

much lessened, women practise to-day, in a more elusive and refined way, the arts which the instinct of self-preservation imposed upon their barbarous ancestresses.

This is, as all will admit, an unpoetical theory, and a revolting one to a chivalrous mind. I, therefore, purposely shield myself behind the great name of Herbert Spencer in reproducing it. Though I do not vouch for it as true, I hold it to be not improbable. A number of unpleasant things will be found in the ancestry of every one of us, if we pursue our researches far enough back; but, in my opinion, they redound to our credit, rather than the contrary, if we convert them into something useful and agreeable. When we consider what malodorous things may have been distilled into the fragrance of the rose and the lily, it is scarcely worth while to regret a remote grandmother's mendacity which in the granddaughter is evaporated into an archness and witchery, lending charm to her speech and a more exquisite flavor to her personality. I feel in such a case positively grateful to the grandmother for having hoodwinked her lord, and do not question the ability of the fair descendant to do the same, though without coming into conflict with a single commandment of the Decalogue. The blunt command, "Thou shalt not," was, I suspect, meant for men rather than for women; for I have known some highly-developed members of the sex who have been able to wind in and out among the ten fatal prohibitions, coming dangerously near some of them, but without getting entangled in any. There is to them a rare pleasure in this hazardous play—which again hints at an inherited complexity of character, never wholly comprehensible to men.

I have remarked that the necessity for duplicity of the cruder sort has lessened and is constantly lessening. But it has not altogether vanished. So long as marriage remains the normal fate of women, the vast majority of them will and must endeavor to make themselves pleasing to men. They must consider primarily, not what they would like to be, but what men would like them to be. Because the feminine ideal for the average man is an unindividualized or but faintly individualized creature—a mere personification of the sex, as it were—the majority of girls pay homage to this unworthy ideal by simulating a clinging dependence and a featureless blankness of character. They repress their real selves, or consciously or unconsciously disguise them. Their education, which, in this country as elsewhere, trains them in *seeming* rather than in *being*, does not aim to make pronounced and capable individuals of them (as in the case of boys), but to develop them into the accepted, traditional type of womanhood which is supposed to have the sanction of the Bible and of the experience of the ages. As to the wisdom of this I do not wish at present to express an opinion. There is no doubt that when women do break away from this traditional standard, as more and more of them do, they become more *outrées*, more revolutionary in speech and conduct than men similarly inclined. There is a good reason for this, or several good reasons. If a woman has the courage to aspire to anything beyond the common lot, the world puts her on the defensive, and by its hostile criticism forces her to account for herself, and drives her then by degrees into a more extreme position than she had at first thought of occupying. For the sake of a consistency which we do not demand of others, she is obliged to antagonize doctrines and institutions which she had never before thought of antagonizing, and to define her attitude towards everything under the sun, until she becomes unwholesomely conscious in every breath she draws.

In the countries of Europe there is scarcely an exception to this rule. The woman who is not content to be a mere embodiment of her sex, and who therefore by individual aspiration strives to differentiate herself, is tabooed by the best society and made the target of cheap ridicule. She may, like Florence Nightingale or Sister Dora, be permitted to bear more than her part of the world's burdens, but she is not permitted to aspire for more than her allotted share of its privileges. It is not so very long since similar conditions prevailed in the United States; nay, they do to a certain extent yet prevail. But that a very substantial progress has been made here is nevertheless certain. Our social conditions afford a wider scope for individual development than do those of Europe. One of the first observations which the English or German traveller is apt to make after landing in New York, is that American women have more vivacity, more character, more freedom of speech and manners than the women of England or Germany. That is but another way of saying that they are more individualized. They have a more distinct, and as a rule a more piquant, flavor of personality. They are not merely specimens of the feminine gender more or less attractive, and labelled for the sake of convenience Minnie, Jennie, or Fannie, but they are primarily Minnie and Jennie and Fannie (though I could wish they had nobler and more dignified appellations), endowed with and modified by their feminine gender. It follows from this that the types of women are here more varied and more pronounced than in Europe; and if an experience of twenty-five years, devoted to discreet observation and sympathetic study, gives me a right to judge, I should like to disburden my note-books of some more or less pretentious sketches which are beginning to rebel against their obscurity.

The first woman whose acquaintance I made in the United States (in 1869) was a very pretty Western girl, who took a peculiar pleasure in saying and doing things which she knew would shock my European notions of propriety. She was slangy in her speech, careless in her pronunciation, and bent upon "having a good time" without reference to the prohibitions which are framed for the special purpose of annoying women. I was sometimes in danger of misinterpreting her conduct, but soon came to the conclusion that there was no harm in her. She ruled her father and her mother, who sometimes interposed feeble objections to her plans for her own and my amusement; but the end invariably was that a puzzled assent was yielded to all her proceedings. She had about as much idea of propriety (in the European sense) as a cat has of mathematics. She recognized no law except her own sovereign will, and her demands were usually so emphatic that no one could disagree with her without the risk of quarrelling. Patriotic she was—bristling with combativeness if a criticism was made which implied disrespect of American manners or institutions. She was good-natured, generous to a fault, and brimming with energy.

This young girl is the type of American womanhood which has become domesticated in European fiction. She is to French, English, and German authors the American type *par excellence*. She is a familiar figure in the French drama, and her pistol-firing and her amusing rowdyism relieve the monotony of many a dull novel. Ouida has caricatured her in *Moths* and Sardou in *L'Oncle Sam*. Henry James ventured some years ago to publish a mild edition of her in *Daisy Miller*, and outraged patriotism denounced him as a slanderer of his country, declaring that he had libelled American womanhood. I, too, in a recent novel, was tempted to make a little literary capital out of my early acquaintance with this personification of the

Declaration of Independence.* I was told by a chorus of reviewers (and I suspected the soprano note in most of them) that the type was one of my own invention; that it did not exist except in my jaundiced eye; that, if it did exist, I had outrageously caricatured it; and that I had conclusively proved myself an alien, devoid of sympathy with the American character. Now, I had prided myself on having avoided the farcical exaggerations of my European *confrères*. I had imagined that my "emancipated young woman" was strictly true to life, and that no single trait of her vivacious personality had been set down in malice or for the sake of effect.

It would seem odd indeed, considering the fact that the novelists of all foreign countries have pounced upon this type as being peculiarly American, if the type had no existence. Such unanimity in misrepresentation would scarcely be conceivable, unless they had come together with malice aforethought and agreed among themselves as to how they were

---

* Delia Saunders in *The Light of Her Countenance.*

to blacken the character of cisatlantic womanhood. But if I had been a party to such a dastardly plot, I dare say I should have forfeited my domestic peace long ago; for I have furnished the most incontestable proof possible that I am a stranger to the sentiments which animate these wretched traducers. I may, therefore, perhaps, be permitted to remark that it need not argue disloyalty to the Constitution if a novelist refuses to depict *couleur de rose* everything he sees. The independent young *Américaine* who pleases herself without reference to the tastes of others, is not a wholly agreeable phenomenon; but it is of no use to deny her existence. She is very prevalent in Europe; and though she rarely invades the so-called best society of our seaboard cities, you need only go abroad or sufficiently far west to find her in all her glory.

The best society, it may be observed in parenthesis, is not the best place to study American types. The highest civilization is hostile to types. It tends towards uniformity of manners, rubs off angularities of conduct, obliterates glaring characteristics. At first glance, a New York afternoon tea does not differ strikingly from a London afternoon tea. In both places people go to show themselves, half out of vanity, half as a matter of duty. They have no expectation of being amused, nor are they amused; but they depart with the amiable fiction upon their lips that they have had "such a delightful time." A certain well-bred hypocrisy is absolutely necessary to make social intercourse smooth and agreeable. It is one of the last results of civilization. The blunt sincerity of the frontiersman stamps him as a barbarian. Women of the Sarah Althea Hill variety flourish yet in the extreme West, and are typical of a semi-barbarous social condition. They are glaring illustrations of our social history which reveal more than would a hundred pages of eloquent text. But even in California that type of woman has ceased to excite admiration; and when it is no longer admired it will soon become extinct. I have heard Californians declare that it never had any existence except in the newspapers; and of course I meekly acquiesced, knowing that Californians carry an incontrovertible argument in their hip pockets. But leaving that question an open one, it is safe to assert that the standard of conduct which demands self-restraint and repression of picturesque eccentricities is slowly travelling westward, and will ere long make us sigh for the dear old days of romance immortalized by Bret Harte and by the dime novel.

There is, however, a type of American womanhood, by no means devoid of cis-atlantic flavor, which has nothing to fear from the march of civilization. She is indeed an agent of civilization and a most powerful one. I met her for the first time in 1869, and have been meeting her daily ever since. Though she may object to the name, I shall call her the Aspiring Woman. As a rule she is not handsome, and she is not conspicuous for taste in dress. She regards dress and all other things which have no bearing upon her intellectual development as being of slight consequence. It would be impossible to arouse her enthusiasm for a French bonnet, and the shrill little ejaculations of rapture in which other women compass a world of meaning (or the opposite) are not found in her vocabulary. She rebukes you with a glance of mild reprobation if you indulge in "frivolous talk" or refer to any physical traits in a member of her sex. There is no affectation in this; it is rather the result of a long puritanic descent, and amounts to a second conscience. She knows the flesh only as something to be mortified, and though she may have abandoned the scriptural grounds for the mortification, she is, in the midst of her consciousness of evil, so good as almost to be able to dispense with the commandments. I have known her skeptical and I have known her religious; but skepticism sat lightly upon her, like a divestible garment, and could not conceal her innate goodness. She is frequently anæmic, and in New England inclines to be flat-chested. The vigor of her physical life usually leaves much to be desired; the poverty of diet in ascetic ancestors has often reduced her vitality, making her undervalue the concerns of the flesh, and overvalue the relative importance of the things of the spirit. I purposely qualify these statements, and do not represent them as being invariably true. The aspiring woman is so extensive and numerous a species that it naturally embraces many varieties. The variety I have described is a conspicuous one, but it is not the only one. There is one trait, however, which they all have in common: they are all bent upon improving themselves, in season and out of season. When they indulge in anything frivolous, it is always from a utilitarian motive. Thus I remember once dancing a waltz with an aspiring young woman. It was at the Cornell University, at the season when the all-absorbing topic is the graduating thesis. Just as we swung out upon the floor she exploded this query in my ears: "Now, won't you be kind enough to give me, just in a few words, the gist of Spinoza's 'Ethics'?" It did not surprise me afterwards to learn that she danced because it was good for the digestion. And her dancing was what might have been expected; it was a conscientious exercise. At every bar of the music she emphasized the time with a jerk, as if she were trying to help me along.

If there is any single trait which radically distinguishes American society, as a whole, from European society, it is a universal hopefulness and aspiration. The European Philistine, though he may not be content with his lot, rarely thinks of rising above the station to which he was born. Society appears so fixed and unyielding that it seems like presumption on his part to defy its prejudice. It requires a very exceptional courage, therefore, and talents of a high order, to aspire successfully. But in the United States aspiration is the rule, not the exception. The man who is content to remain what he is, who does not expect to rise to some dizzy height of wealth or of fame, was until recently a *rara avis* in the Western States. And as for the young women, they were animated by an ambition which in many cases was pathetic. I met, during my sojourn in Ohio and Illinois, daughters of farmers and mechanics who were cultivating themselves in secret, groping their way most pitifully, without help or guidance, and often gulping the most abominable stuff under the impression that they were being intellectually nourished.

The young woman who cultivates poetry under the most distressing circumstances, and perhaps finally publishes a pitiful little volume at her own expense, is a butt for newspaper ridicule; but to me she is a pathetic character. If there were not in her a spark of the Promethean fire, she would not expend so much vital energy and deluded hope, in the face of many discouragements, on her clumsy or insipid rhymes. She may, indeed, be a conceited pretender; but the probabilities are nine to one that she is something better. Having had no opportunities for culture beyond such as the district school offers, she has, of course, no chance of succeeding. A utilitarian would advise her to throw her verses into the fire, to tuck up her skirts, and to help her mother scrub, darn, and wash dishes. Such a counsellor would be worthy of attention. But, in the first place, he would find that the mother would object to the help (for she is, as a rule, proud of her daughter's unusual accomplishments); and, secondly, something valuable would vanish out of American life, if all the misguided and largely futile aspiration were lost which constitutes the tragedy and the dignity of thousands of narrow, toilsome lives. When the failure is, at last, tacitly acknowledged and the hope of success abandoned, something yet remains, which is beyond the reach of hostile critics and an indifferent public. This may be a mere heightened self-respect, with a touch of defiance, or it may be the lifting of the character to a higher plane than it would have reached without the futile aspiration. Women who have passed through an experience of this sort transfer, when they become mothers, their ambition to their children, and will make any sacrifice in the hope of enabling their sons to attain what they missed. It is a priceless blessing to a man to have had such a mother; and all over this country they are scattered in log-huts and farm-houses, in tenements and in brown-stone fronts.

I have often endeavored, after each

return from a European pilgrimage, to make clear to myself wherein the charm of American women consists. I do not mean the mere charm of womanhood, for that is universal; but something superadded, depending upon climate and social conditions, which lends to it a heightened flavor, a more exquisite bouquet. I have always sympathized with the perverter of Pope who declared that the noblest study of mankind is woman; and of all womankind no variety better repays sympathetic and discriminating study than the American. For the purposes of the sociologist no less than those of the novelist, women are unquestionably more interesting than men; and in particular, American women are more interesting than American men. As a leisured class (comparatively speaking), they have more time to cultivate the amenities of life than have their husbands and brothers. They read more; and a larger proportion than will be found anywhere else in the world have interests beyond dress and social tittle-tattle. Some few have vigorous, well-trained intellects, and naturally feel their superiority to the majority of men with whom they associate. They then rashly conclude that women, as a rule, are the intellectual superiors of men, or would be if the same opportunities of education were afforded them; and presently we find them in woman-suffrage conventions, petitioning legislatures and agitating for social reform. Far be it from me to throw ridicule upon these heroic protagonists, or to underestimate the value of their labors. Though I do not sympathize with some of their aims, I cannot but admire their intrepidity, their fortitude, their noble enthusiasm. The influence of their work is good, and we could ill afford to dispense with it. It is not to be denied, however, that they forfeit much of that charm which, in the present condition of the world, constitutes to the benighted male the chief attraction of the sex.

I believe there is inherent in all women what may be called, without any invidious inference, a yearning for the commonplace — for the normal lot. Those who protest most strenuously against the injustice of society to their sex, are as a rule willing to exchange their uncomfortable prominence for the contented obscurity of a domestic hearth. If it were possible to explore their innermost hearts, I believe it would be found that they have an underlying respect, not to say fondness, for the tyranny which they justly denounce. Madame de Staël's willingness to exchange all her fame and intellectual superiority for Madame de Récamier's gift of pleasing, is the most profoundly womanly trait recorded of that brilliant amazon. In the correspondence of George Eliot, too, there is a regretful acceptance of the eminence that is thrust upon her; and in her personal life a kind of reversed aspiration is perceptible, a yearning for the ordinary ties of ordinary women—for love, dependence, self-surrender. The apparent aberrations of her career are easily accounted for on this hypothesis.

As regards this fundamental characteristic, American women do not differ from their sisters the world over. The point in which they do differ is chiefly a certain intellectual alertness, an adaptability, a readiness to apply their minds quickly to any new topic, a mental resonance which responds promptly to a deft touch. This accounts largely for the charm they exercise over foreigners. The proportion of truly delightful women, well-bred, sympathetic, and intelligent, is larger in the best society of our great cities than in society of a corresponding grade in England, France, or Germany. In stateliness, dignity, and finish of manner, the aristocracy of the old world naturally excel them; but it is marvellous to observe the readiness with which, when they marry noblemen, they adapt themselves to their new surroundings and beat "the daughters of a hundred earls" on their own ground. They become *grandes dames* in an incredibly short time, yet without losing their American cleverness, delicacy, and piquancy of style. Some of the grandest ladies one meets in Vienna, Paris, Berlin, and London, the sight of whom awakens a sneaking admiration for feudalism and a dim disloyalty to the Declaration of Independence, turn out, on inquiry, to be transplanted American heiresses. And yet no one would have believed, without proof to the contrary, that this combination of graciousness and dignity, these delicate gradations of cordiality and reserve, this consummate skill in dealing with nice questions of etiquette, could have sprung from the soil of democracy.

American ladies at home, though their native tact usually comes to their rescue, rarely possess in the same degree this adroitness. We have not yet gotten through the imitative stage in our social customs and observances, and no one who has an alien model in view can behave with perfect naturalness and security. The English yoke sits heavily upon that part of New York society which claims to be "the best," and upon the girls in particular. That distressing handshake, with the elbow raised at an angle of ninety degrees, is one of the recent importations. The rule not to introduce, for which we are also indebted to London, is another heavy incubus, which strangles conversation and produces awkwardness and misery. But the women who make it a point to be abreast of London in all these more or less arbitrary observances are apparently unaware that they are robbing themselves of their highest charm when they are no longer frankly American. It is their national flavor, refined by intelligence and culture, which makes them a power both at home and abroad; and they should have the courage to be proud of this nationality, and to show their pride in it by abandoning their attitude of social dependence upon Great Britain.

1890

GERMAN AND AMERICAN WOMEN

CYNICAL friend of mine, who is a bachelor, once made an observation which clings like a burr to my memory. It had always appeared a significant circumstance to him, he said, that God, when "he saw all that he had made, and, behold, it was very good," had not yet created woman. After her appearance upon the scene, the goodness of creation might be rationally questioned. At all events, the Bible is silent on the subject.

I ought, perhaps, to add that my cynical friend is a German, and that, if he had been an American, he would — well, he would not have had the courage of his conviction. He would never have dared to utter so heterodox an opinion. The United States, as we all know, is the women's paradise, and they have a thousand ingenious ways of making life a burden to the man who has the audacity not to admire them. I would rather that a millstone were tied about my neck, and that I were sunk in the depths of the sea, than court the terrors of such a fate. Therefore I shield myself judiciously behind the back of my cynical friend, with whose opinions, I beg to state, I have not the remotest sympathy. I dare say he had been jilted, which, to the feminine mind, is a sufficient cause for all vagaries of conduct and sentiment. However, it may be urged as an ameliorating circumstance, that (though a German-American) he had known chiefly his own countrywomen, and the few specimens of the American woman with whom he had come in contact had been of that nomadic species which one meets in second-class family hotels and boarding-houses. I don't blame any man for questioning the rationality of creation after having been doomed, for four years, to such companionship. But, of course, I was too chivalrous to make such an admission to this

Teutonic traducer of American womanhood; and accordingly I found myself launched, before long, in a hot debate on the comparative merits of German and American women. To quote it verbatim would be an endless task; but it had the effect of stimulating my mind to grapple with this subject—and it is terrible what an amount of reflection may be expended upon it without the least palpable result. I shall, however, venture to present a few vague and extremely shadowy conclusions, from which I shall instantly recede, if any fair reader objects to them. And she—the fair reader—will kindly bear in mind that all that is uncomplimentary to her sex in the following dissertation is due to the jaundiced cynicism of my crude Teutonic friend; while all of which she may be pleased to approve is due solely and exclusively to my own genial and intelligent observation.

Well, then, the American society girl (*cynicus loquitur*) is brought up without any adequate sense of duty. She is made to believe or to infer from the attitude of her environment, that the chief business

of life is to amuse one's self; and that the
day is to be counted as lost which does
not afford some new pleasurable excitement. Mothers, who have themselves
known the inestimable discipline of hard-
ship and toil, have a natural desire to
make their daughters' youth brighter and
happier than was their own; and by this
generous motive they are impelled to introduce a ruinous laxity into their relations with their children. The dear girls
must have a good time, at all hazards;
and their pleasure and convenience must
be consulted above all else. The father
and the mother sacrifice themselves to
this end, and fondly imagine that they
are furthering their daughters' welfare by
removing every stone out of their path.
As a consequence, they rear beautiful
little monsters of selfishness and con-
ceit, who at the proper age trip sweet-
ly into matrimony with a thousand demands, and without the least conception
of the serious duties which that relation
imposes upon them. When the husband
fails to subordinate himself (as he is very
apt to do) with the same willingness as

papa and mamma did, to the whims and caprices of his young wife—particularly if he fails to provide amusements enough, regardless of expense—then follow weeping and wailing and possibly also gnashing of teeth; little scenes are enacted (in strict privacy at first) in which neither party is apt to appear to advantage; and trouble rises, like à great blood-red moon, with an ominous face, on the matrimonial horizon. The postulate that women should be independent and the equals of men sounds eminently fair. But when two such independents marry, they are sure to get into collision. One or the other must surrender a portion of his independence, or retire from the partnership. It is a most deplorable fact that so many choose the latter alternative, and thereby do their share towards undermining the foundations of society. Men and women are no less fit, by nature, for the married state here than elsewhere; but the utterly lax and slipshod education, more particularly of young women, is responsible for the ruin which overtakes so large a percentage of American households. I am —

that is to say, my German friend was—old-fashioned enough to believe that there are no privileges which do not also involve duties; and that it is far more important to impress a young person, of either sex, with a consciousness of the latter than of the former. I never knew any one, breathing the air of our democracy, who did not, without much guidance, discover what society owed to him; but I have known a great many who had only the dimmest notions of their own obligations towards society.

Now, in Germany, the situation is, in some respects, exactly the opposite. There women have the acutest perception of the very things which American women largely lack. They are trained from childhood in ideas which we regard as mediæval, and from which we emancipated ourselves in 1789 or thereabouts. First, the German maidens regard wifehood and motherhood as their legitimate vocation; and they have a veritable horror of anything that savors of "woman's rights." They do not ask for the omission of the "obey" from the marriage service (as a fair friend of mine did); nor do they interpret it in a Pickwickian sense, as another charming damsel of my acquaintance professed to have done, when she was reminded of the odious little verbs which she had been beguiled into uttering. Ah, but the German women—what else can you expect of them? They are so palpably inferior to their husbands; and moreover, they dress atrociously, remarks a soprano voice at my elbow. Granted. They are far less complex than their American sisters; they are less highly developed; they have not (unless they are very high up in the social scale) half the alertness of mind, facility of address, or independence of thought. They are bound by a rigid social tradition, which our women repudiate. They glory in their domestic martyrdom, their sacrifice of self, their loving and conscientious performance of their duties to husband and children. But, although one may admit that they are not individually as charming as American women in the corresponding social position, it is a question which admits of different replies, whether they do not, other things being equal, make better wives and better mothers than—than—the ladies on the planet Jupiter. The sentiment of home, which is chiefly fostered by the mother, certainly exists in a higher and intenser degree in Germany than it does here; the domestic ties mean more, and are regarded with a deeper respect. Look at Kaulbach's illustrations to Schiller's *Song of the Bell*, and you will see how they are permeated with this sentiment of the sanctity of home, and what a tender poetic afflatus dignifies and ennobles all the typical incidents of family life. What can be lovelier than the cartoon entitled "The Mother's Instruction," which exhales a breath of all that is sweetest and best in the German Fatherland? I wish it were natural to exclaim, at the sight of such a scene, "How American!" instead of being obliged to say, "How German!"

The fundamental trait of German womanhood is—not intellectual brilliancy, not readiness of resource or practical sense, but self-sacrificing goodness of heart.

We who are accustomed to more highly-flavored peculiarities are inclined to misjudge this kind of quiet, unobtrusive goodness, and so undervalue the sterling virtues which it conceals. But what alienates us still more is a certain sentimental effusiveness and exuberance of feeling, which lie as remote as possible from the Anglo-Saxon temperament. What we fear above all things is to make ourselves ridiculous; and every exhibition of emotion has to us, unhappily, a lurking suggestion of the ridiculous. We, therefore, repress ourselves until we are in danger of becoming insincere and unnatural from sheer dread of compromising our precious dignity. Now, the Germans, and particularly the German women, are never in the least troubled with this question of the ridiculous. They have, I verily believe, a depression in their craniums where the bump of humor ought to have been situated; which, of course, saves a deal of discomfort. But, as a compensation, they possess the correlative virtue in which our society women, both old and young, are conspicuously lacking. I mean a capacity for seriousness. What can be more distressing to a man, who has outgrown his first, callow youth, than the perpetual chaff and banter in which he is expected to indulge in his intercourse with ladies? I have felt positively murderous at times, after having spent an evening in the company of fair enchantresses, who insisted upon being funny and seeing a lurking joke in every remark which I uttered. Now, I dare say I enjoy a good joke as much as any one; but humor, which affords a delightful seasoning to conversation, becomes distasteful and unwholesome as a steady diet. Forced jesting, coupled with that nervous, half-hysterical vivacity which we all know so well, serves but to disguise poverty of thought. It is either because our young women have no capacity for serious thinking, or because they distrust the capacity which they possess, that they seek refuge in this imbecile jocularity.

I am speaking, of course, of society women; for I am well aware that, in the strata below, the humorous aspect of life is in no danger of predominating.

Nor am I blind to the fact that, within the society which I am criticising, there are many lovely and brilliant women, who incline me to thank God daily for the privilege of having been born their contemporary. But these are radiant exceptions which prove the rule. An overwhelming majority of the women who figure at routs, dinners, and balls seem shallow in heart and brain; and they lack, moreover, that supreme charm of womanly dignity which covers all minor imperfections with a mantle of grace. They dress extremely well; far better than a similar assemblage would be likely to do in any other part of the world. They are superficially clever, and adapt themselves with great readiness to any situation. But you will find, if you penetrate beneath their outer armor of conventionality, a certain dryness and poverty of nature, a comparative absence of those warm, sweet, fundamentally womanly qualities which are the strength and the glory of womanhood; and in their stead a host of petty and obtrusive little vanities; a grim, hard-headed selfishness and worldly calculation, which is determined to get the most out of life with the least possible sacrifice; and an essential flimsiness of character which makes them incapable of noble motives and disinterested actions. This is the sort of women whose lives are filled with so-called social duties; *i. e.*, visiting, personal gossip, strife for precedence, snubs to supposed inferiors, flattering attention to superiors, and vain and mean ambitions that would scarcely seem worth the expenditure of one-tenth of the energy which they demand. They go to church, too, chiefly as a matter of form, and figure conspicuously among the patrons of fashionable charities. But the spirit which should sanctify the deed is so glaringly absent, that the deed itself loses whatever virtue it might otherwise possess.

It is the system of education to which I have alluded, or rather the lack of system, which is responsible for the prevalence of this type. It is the combination of lax indulgence and neglect on the part of the parents — indulgence as regards material comforts, and neglect as regards spiritual guidance and the training of character — which produces these fair, heartless sirens, whom we meet at Newport, Bar Harbor, and Narragansett Pier, whose shrill song is, however, apt to allure to perdition only men of their own species, unless indeed they be very young.

Now, my cynical friend (whose opinions I have been quoting) has the audacity to maintain that the women in the upper strata of German society are finer and nobler specimens of their sex than American women of the corresponding position. (I have long been pondering whether I ought to challenge him to fight with pistols or with swords, unless he consents to withdraw this offensive remark; and as I shoot better than I fence, I am slowly gravitating towards the more deadly weapon. In the meanwhile, I am in hopes that he will repent of his rudeness and recant.) But, as I was saying, he has the hardihood to insinuate that the German girls of to-day, themselves the result of conscientious education and often of stern discipline, are more impressive phenomena in their blonde innocence and Spartan simplicity of life than our pretty, flimsy, pampered, and self-willed daughters of wealth and enervating luxury. These girls, he says, will make noble mothers, and happy are the sons whom they shall tenderly guide with affectionate severity and far-seeing love to a pure and vigorous manhood. Of course, distance has lent its enchantment to this picture and is, in part, responsible for its poetic tint. There is this to be said, on the other side, that a man has to make his choice among these girls largely on trust; for, with all their virtues, they are a trifle insipid, until wifehood and motherhood have awakened their latent characteristics. They are distressingly alike, both in their outward type and in their sentiments; and they rarely develop an interesting individuality until after marriage, or after they have given up the expectation of marriage. For the male species as we all know, are afraid of anything of definite complexion, preferring a mere personification of the venerable and traditional qualities which are supposed to be inherent in the sex. The German male would even count it a gain if he could arrest all individual development in his wife for an indefinite period. And it is inevitable that this ideal of blankness, feebly tinted by a few traditional virtues, will be reflected in the mind and demeanor of German girlhood. For when the penalty of not conforming to this ideal is celibacy, women will strive to appear what men want them to be. But, in spite of this effort at self-obliteration, there are women in Germany who are as pronounced personalities as Bismarck or Von Moltke. I recall one, the wife of a celebrated professor and political leader, with whose acquaintance I would not have dispensed for a small fortune. To see her sit at her table, tall, blond, and stately, surrounded by her sons and daughters, who loved and almost revered her, was a picture never to be forgotten. The father, though he was a man of exceptional gifts and absorbed in public affairs, seemed to me almost dwarfed by his wife. Her sweet, maternal dignity, her innate courtesy, her easy flow of interesting conversation, made her seem to me the noblest type of a matron I had ever beheld, and she revealed to me, incidentally, an ideal of family life which remains to this day something unattainable. Though she was the dominant force in the household, she deferred to her husband with a loving delight in submission which was beautiful to witness. She was proud of him and missed no opportunity to make her children proud of him. And she seemed utterly unconscious that she was herself exceptional, unless it were for her good-fortune in being the wife of such a husband and the mother of so many fine children. Let me add that she was intensely Prussian in sentiment, loyal to the core, and an admirer of Bismarck. If she had been a contemporary of Plutarch, he would have included her eventless life among his heroic biographies.

My domestic critic, to whom I have read the above, declares her disapprobation in general, and calls my attention to the fact that all generalizations must contain a modicum of error. It is because I cheerfully grant this proposition that I finish this study of odious comparisons, not with a generalization, but with a portrait. Whether I have succeeded in holding the scales of international justice even I do not know; nor do I pretend to be wholly unbiassed. But my prejudice (though you may find it hard to believe) is in favor of America and whatever is American.

1891

THE AMERICAN NOVELIST
AND HIS PUBLIC

IT is said that poets are born, not made. The same assertion might be hazarded, with equal truth, of lawyers, engineers, doctors, and clergymen; in fact, of any man eminent in his profession. The great ones are born, the little ones are only made. Marked inherited ability in a definite direction is, however, no sure guarantee of greatness. Circumstances must do the rest. The man is the resultant of his environment and his heredity; if they impel him in the same direction, he will get far; if they push in opposite directions and counteract each other, he may not get anywhere. The one is as important as the other. A man's heredity he has to accept as an unalterable fact; he can do nothing to improve or modify it; though I believe the time will come when society will awake to a sense of its responsibility and prevent unions which must result in vicious or diseased offspring. As regards environment, we have already accepted the responsibility. In our power to change and modify it so as to serve a definite purpose, we have, if not our own fates, at least those of our children, partly in our hands. Much is, of course, yet beyond our power of calculation; but much, also, within it. The late Anthony Trollope's idea, that a young man could be trained to be a novelist, as he might for the legal or medical profession, is, therefore, not so absurd as it has been represented to be. Supposing the young man to be of a little more than average cleverness, he would have as good a chance of success in that field as in that of law or medicine. He could not, perhaps, go to work deliberately accumulating experience, but he could, by a process similar to that which Goethe employed in his own conscious self-development, educate himself by travel and study, and sharpen his faculties of observation. He might not become great by this process, but if success were conditioned by greatness, how many of us would indeed achieve it? That greatness may even be a barrier to success is demonstrated by the posthumous celebrity of many an author, who asked for bread and received a stone.

The public makes its authors in its own image and likeness. It demands a certain article and it gets it. The man who suits the average taste is the successful man. There is, to be sure, such a thing as educating your public; but the process is slow and expensive. The public which is capable of being educated is never very large, though it is apt to make up in devotion for what it lacks in numbers. The authors, however, who are satisfied with this limited renown are exceptional; the great majority of them hunger for popularity. For the attainment of this a benevolent chorus is an important aid. The journalistic friends of the novelist conspire to advertise him, in season and out of season, and treat his greatness as an article of faith; and he, in return, pushes their fortunes whenever the chance presents itself.

If this were, however, the severest symptom of the hunger for popularity, it would be no serious matter; the influence of these little cliques is, after all, limited; and there are plenty of reputations among us which have grown healthily without such artificial tending. But there are other forces at work, in our literature, which are more permanently injurious. Chief among these I hold to be the fact that the American public, as far as the novelist is concerned, is the female half of it. The readers of novels are chiefly young girls, and a popular novel is a novel which pleases them. If an American author should attempt to write fiction for men, his books would share the fate of Rousseau's "Ode to Posterity," which never reached its address. The average American has no time to read anything but newspapers, while his daughters have an abundance of time at their disposal, and a general disposition to employ it in anything that is amusing. The novelist who has begun to realize that these young persons constitute his public, naturally endeavors to amuse them. He knows, in a general way, what ladies like, and as the success of his work depends upon his hitting their taste, he makes a series of small concessions to it, which, in the end, determines the character of his book. He feels that he is conversing with ladies and not with men, and his whole attitude, his style, and the topics he selects for discussion, suffer the change which is implied in this circumstance. He discusses dress with elaborate minuteness, and enters, with a truly feminine enthusiasm, into the mysteries of the toilet. He shuns large questions and problems because his audience is chiefly interested in small questions and problems. He avoids everything which requires thought, because, rightly or wrongly, thought is not supposed to be the ladies' *forte*. Their education has not trained them for independent reflection. They are by nature conservative, and have been told by their pastors and teachers that the so-called modern ideas are dangerous and improper to discuss. Accordingly, the novelist who aspires for their favor becomes, also, conservative, and refrains from discussing what, according to the boarding-school standard, is unsafe or improper.

This silence concerning all the vital things of life, and the elaborate attention paid to things of small consequence, I believe to be the most serious defect in the present American fiction. The strong forces which are visibly and invisibly at work in our society, fashioning our destinies as a nation, are to a great extent ignored by our novelists. Politics, for instance, which, outside of the great cities, plays so large a part in the lives of our people, is, out of deference to the ladies, rarely allowed to invade our novels. In all the tales of Howells and James, which are typical of the tendencies of the time, I do not remember a single political incident — unless, indeed, the flirtations of the capricious Christina with the little socialistic bookbinder in *Princess Casamassima* may be termed a political incident. Mr. Marion Crawford had, to be sure, once the hardihood to advertise his misinformation concerning the politics of his native land in a book entitled *An American Politician*, but I doubt if he expected any one to take such a performance seriously. J. W. De Forest published, some ten or twelve years ago, an excellent political novel, showing abundant insight; but *Honest John Vane* can scarcely have reaped the success it deserved, since the author soon afterwards abandoned the field of fiction, and has, as far as I know, never since been heard from. In Edward Eggleston's *Roxy* there are admirable episodes from the Harrison and Tyler campaign of 1840, and in *The Hoosier Schoolmaster* politics also holds its due proportion of space and interest. But these exceptions are sufficiently rare to prove the rule, that the novelist of to-day avoids politics. Of the anonymous novel, *Democracy*, I have not spoken, because it was not what it purported to be—a characterization of life at our national capital—but a distorting and malevolent satire on it; and Albion J. Tourgée's *A Fool's Errand* and *Bricks Without Straw* were so strongly colored by vindictive partisanship as to be campaign documents rather than contributions to literature.

I am aware that it is ungracious, on the part of a man who has written novels, to find fault with those who have had the kindness to read his productions. It would be perfectly fair if they should answer him: "If we had not been your public you would have had none; if we had not bought your books they would have remained on the shelves of your publisher. Whatever you are, or pretend to be, in a literary capacity, you owe to us." As I have said, I am painfully aware that such a reply would be in order, and I scarcely know what to say to clear myself of the charge of ingratitude. My only plea is that I care more for American literature than for the small figure I may happen to cut in it. I confess I have never written a book without helplessly deploring the fact that young ladies were to be the arbiters of its fate; that young persons whose opinions on any other subject, involving the need of thought or experience, we should probably hold in light esteem, constitute collectively an Areopagus from whose judgments, in matters relating to fiction, there is no appeal. To be a purveyor of amusement (especially if one suspects that he has the stuff in him for something better) is not at all amusing. To be obliged to repress that which is best in him, and offer that which is of slight consequence, is the plight to which many a novelist, in this paradise of women, is reduced. Nothing less is demanded of him by that inexorable force called public taste, as embodied in the editors of the paying magazines, behind whom sits, arrayed in stern and bewildering loveliness, his final judge, the young American girl. She is the Iron Madonna who strangles in her fond embrace the American novelist; the Moloch upon whose altar he sacrifices, willingly or unwillingly, his chances of greatness. In the vast majority of cases in which the chances do not exist, there is, of course, no sacrifice. But in the cases where they do exist there is a distinct half-unconscious lowering of standard, a distinct descent to a lower plane of thought or thoughtlessness. A weak lemonade mixture, harmless and mildly exhilarating, adapted for the palates of *ingénues*, is poured out in a steady stream from our presses, and we all drink it, and, from patriotic motives, declare it to be good. When, however, we read a novel like Tolstoï's *Anna Karénina* or Daudet's *Le Nabab* we appreciate, perhaps, the difference between a literature addressed to girls and a literature intended for men and women.

I am by no means blind to the fact that we have among us the beginning of what promises to be a sounder and more serious school of fiction. Mr. Howells deserves, in my opinion, the thanks of all lovers of literature for his frank and fearless attacks, both by precept and example, upon the worn-out romantic ideals. As long as it is expected of the novelist that he shall spin ingenious and entertaining yarns, his art is not bound by the laws of reality, and is free to degenerate into all sorts of license. As long as a crude public taste found more pleasure in the abnormal than the normal, the popular novelist was forced, like Wilkie Collins

and Gaboriau, to ransack the records of
police courts and lunatic asylums in
search of startling incidents; and the
novel swarmed with villains and their
victims. As a picture of life, such fiction
was worse than worthless. It exists, of
course, yet, and has a large public; but
it is, in great part, due to Mr. Howells
that readers who lay claim to literary culture are now beginning to repudiate it.
His long series of novels in the *Atlantic*,
the *Century*, and *Harper's Magazine*, have
dealt uniformly with American themes,
and have drawn within the domain of
fiction hitherto unexplored types and
phases of our national life. In *A Hazard
of New Fortunes* and *The Rise of Silas
Lapham* he has penetrated more deeply
into the heart of reality, as it manifests
itself on this side of the Atlantic, than
any previous novelist, and has made it
easier for those who shall follow after him
to rely upon insight, style, and knowledge of the world for success, and to
dispense with the crude devices of the
sensationalist. If he has not, like Zola
and Clarétie in France, and Spielhagen

and Freytag in Germany, undertaken to grapple with the social problems of the day, this may be in part due to a temperamental aversion for polemics, and partly to the training which the monthly magazine gives to all its contributors, keeping them in the safe track of uncontested generalities.* The editor, being anxious to keep all his old subscribers and secure new ones, requires of his contributor that he shall offend no one. He must not expose a social or religious sham, because there are hundreds, if not thousands, of subscribers who believe in this sham, and would stop the magazine if it were attacked. If he takes up a particular phase of life, he must steer carefully, so as to step on nobody's toes, and if he has extreme beliefs and convictions, take good care to keep them in proper restraint. I am not applying this to Mr. Howells, who is sufficiently outspoken in his convictions, but to every novelist

---

* Since the above was written Mr. Howells has published *Letters from Altruria*, in which he does show the keenest appreciation of the problems of American society.

who reaches his public through the medium of the monthly magazines. However much he may rebel against it, he is forced to chew the cud of old ideas, and avoid espousing any cause which lacks the element of popularity. If he is of an ardent temperament, he must curb his ardor, except in the love-scenes, where he is permitted to be discreetly passionate. If, like so many of the world's best poets, he is in advance of his time; if he is a non-conformist in respect to any commonly accepted practice or belief, he has but the choice of suppressing his convictions or remaining silent. He must offer that part of himself which he believes to be of small consequence, and conceal that which he believes to be important and vital.

In all the countries of Europe, except England, the literary conditions are, in this respect, very different. There the monthly magazine (without which American authorship scarcely could exist) has not attained the prominence or the development that it has reached in our prosperous democracy. The majority of the

German periodicals appeal to a definite class of readers, and are not afraid of proclaiming (in signed articles) the most tremendous social and religious heresies. Publications like the *Gartenlaube* and *Westermann's Deutsche Monatshefte*, which are especially addressed to the prosperous *bourgeoisie*, exact the same conservatism of their contributors as do our magazines; but the *Deutsche Rundschau* obviously emulates the *Revue des Deux Mondes* in the scope it gives to radical opinions, as long as the literary excellence is sufficient to keep the tale or discussion on a high intellectual plane. The consequence is that the *Gartenlaube* has developed a peculiar kind of female novelist, of which Marlitt, Werner, and Fanny Lewald were the most conspicuous representatives. They are safe, conservative, and romantic; and, accordingly, very popular in translation with the patrons of our circulating libraries. Writers like Spielhagen, Freytag, Wildenbruch, and Sudermann, on the other hand, prefer to seek their first publicity in the *feuilletons* of the daily papers, which impose no restraints upon them in the interest of tender readers. Accordingly, we have in Spielhagen a most vigorous discussion of the great social questions from the point of view of a bold and original thinker; fearless expositions of the influence of the aristocracy upon the State at large and the lower classes; inimitable satires on the official orthodoxy and its exponents, the Lutheran clergy. Everywhere there are vigor, originality, a fresh and contagious radicalism.

In France the supply of excellent fiction so far exceeds the capacity of the few good magazines that the editorial opinion of the latter exerts but a very slight influence upon the novelist, and the daily papers like *Le Temps*, *Le Journal des Debats*, etc., which regularly print fiction in their *feuilletons*, allow a man of recognized ability to say whatever he likes, if he only says it well. The *Revue des Deux Mondes*, indeed, exacts few but literary qualifications of its writers of fiction; and even George Sand, the most gifted and most erratic of social revolutionists, was for five years its most valued contributor. She quarrelled, to be sure, with the *Revue*, started, successively, two periodicals of her own, and found, finally, her sphere in the absolute and congenial unrestraint of the *feuilleton*. Daudet, Zola, and Clarétie likewise revel in the liberty which the daily press allows them, and develop there, for good or for ill, to the full limit of their individualities.

The recent literary history of the Scandinavian countries, where the magazine only exists in a primitive stage of development, shows the same tendency to make the novel the vehicle of advanced thought. All the vital questions of the day, in religion, politics, and society, are being vigorously expounded and debated in works of fiction. Björnson, who launches his books upon the market without the intervention of any paper or periodical, has published a novel (*Flags are Flying in Harbor and City**) in which he introduces successively four generations of the same family, for the purpose of illustrating the psychological and physiologi-

* The English translation is entitled *The Heritage of the Kurts*.

cal laws of heredity in their mutual inter-dependence, and enforcing the moral lessons which are involved therein. Alexander Kielland diagnoses with dispassionate serenity and truth the hidden diseases of the body social, and by his keen and biting satire arouses against himself a storm of denunciation. So far from suffering by thus being made the battle-field of warring thought, the novel gains thereby a breadth and dignity which it never can attain where it is constructed with a sole view to entertainment. The old maxim, *l'art pour l'art*—art for art's sake—originated with the romanticists, and is losing whatever validity it ever had. Art can engage in no better pursuit than to stimulate noble and healthful thought on all matters of human concern, and thereby clear the prejudiced mind and raise the average of human happiness.

1886

THE PROGRESSIVE REALISM
OF AMERICAN FICTION

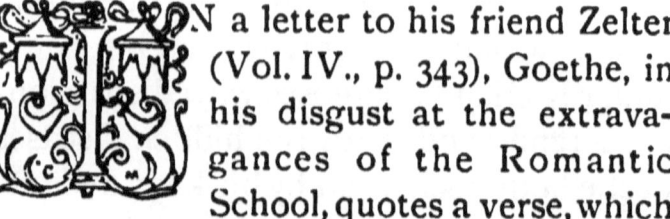N a letter to his friend Zelter (Vol. IV., p. 343), Goethe, in his disgust at the extravagances of the Romantic School, quotes a verse, which he has just written, prophetic of the future of American literature. Although it makes no claim to poetic merit, the sentiment which it expresses is sufficiently remarkable to deserve translation:

America, thy happy lot
Above old Europe's I exalt:
Thou hast no castle ruin hoar
No giant columns of basalt.
Thy soul is not troubled
In living light of day
By useless traditions,
Vain strife and affray.
Grasp but the present that is thine,
And when thy children take to writing,
May kindly Fate preserve their tales
From robbers, knights, and ghosts affrighting.

I fancy Goethe must have been aware when he wrote this verse (June 21, 1827) that the Americans had already taken to writing, and that their famous novelist, James Fenimore Cooper, was treading this very path from which he hoped that kindly Fate would preserve him. Knights and ruined castles he was, to be sure, by the necessities of the case, forced to eschew; but I doubt not that he regarded it as a dire deprivation. Robbers, red and white, are his stock characters, and, if I remember rightly, he also dealt in ghosts. Edgar Allan Poe revelled in horrors, and our other pioneer novelist, Charles Brockden Brown, of Philadelphia, had all the qualities which would have recommended him to Goethe's particular detestation, being slipshod in style and exhibiting a sovereign disregard of reality. His works abound in psychological curiosities and superingenious mysteries, exulting, like those of his romantic compeers, in all the calamities from which in the Prayer Book we ask God to deliver us.

From the romanticism of Brown and

Poe to that of Hawthorne, who chronologically follows the latter as the next notable dispenser of American fiction, we take a long stride forward. Brown's productions belonged to the family of Mrs. Radcliffe and Goodwin, and owned only the airiest allegiance to American soil and climate. Hawthorne, on the other hand, was so distinctly a product of New England blood and environment, that he would have been absolutely inconceivable in any other setting. As he disclaims, however, the title of novelist, preferring that of romancer, it would be unfair to measure him by any standard of mere fidelity to fact.

He says, in the preface to *The House of the Seven Gables:*

"When a writer calls his work a Romance, it need hardly be observed that he wishes to claim a certain latitude, both as to its fashion and material, which he would not have felt entitled to assume had he professed to be writing a novel."

This very romance, however, has, with all its fanciful psychology, so unmistakable a New England flavor as almost to make the disclaimer of the preface superfluous. Though the human conscience, with its mysterious heritage of sin and woe, was his theme, the spiritual climate in which his strange blossoms unfolded their hectic beauty was that of the New World; and with their singular delicacy of form and texture they could never have grown anywhere else. The disadvantages under which he labored as a romancer in a world ostensibly devoid of romance, are strongly, almost amusingly, insisted upon in his preface to *The Marble Faun:*

"No author without a trial can conceive of the difficulty of writing a romance about a country where there is no shadow, no antiquity, no mystery, no picturesque and gloomy wrong, nor anything but a commonplace prosperity, in broad and simple daylight, as is happily the case with my dear native land. Romance and poetry, ivy, lichens, and wall-flowers need ruin to make them grow."

That he was by no means lacking in the sense of the reality is shown by the exquisite delicacy with which he reproduces the atmospheric tone and color of any locality which forms the setting of his more important scenes; and if further testimony is needed, his note-books will furnish it in abundance.

Mrs. Harriet Beecher Stowe, whose popularity reached further than that of any of her predecessors, had no intellectual affinity to Hawthorne; but her kinship with her greater contemporary, Charles Dickens, is unmistakable. Eva, in *Uncle Tom's Cabin*, belongs to the same lachrymose family as Little Nell, and they both die (one might almost say) with the same emotional extravagance. The inimitable drollery and genial satire of Dickens are absent in Mrs. Stowe; but the tearful sentimentalism which exhibits itself in a kind of hysterical pathos they both have in common. The notion I had formed of the negroes from my first perusal of *Uncle Tom's Cabin* was that they were a kind of archangels in black, hounded, tortured, and abused by the fiendish whites on account of their moral superiority. It took me some time and cost me not a little money to correct this impression after my arrival in the United States. Though in all Mrs. Stowe's romances the tendency is perceptible, she has, as she grew older, abandoned much of her early extravagance, which was defensible enough in the cause of reform, and has steered closer and closer to the shores of reality. In *Oldtown Folks*, and particularly in the Sam Lawson sketches, she betrays a power of minute observation and an appreciation of local color which might almost entitle her to the name of a realist.

Another conspicuous representative of the school of Dickens is Bret Harte, who, however, in *Gabriel Conroy*, plays at ducks and drakes with probability in a way that would have given even Dickens a qualm.

It is the first chapter of *Bleak House* which contains the famous description of a London fog, worked up, as it appears to me, to a strained, tensely quivering pitch, when a single more wrench at the screw would snap the string. Where Dickens has fog everywhere, Bret Harte substitutes "snow everywhere," as the season demands, and proceeds to describe it, not with the same words, but in the same key as Dickens, with the same dithyrambic vehemence. The rhetorical cadence of the two passages is so strikingly similar that I cannot forbear to quote. Here is Dickens:

"Fog everywhere. Fog up the river, where it flows among green aits and meadows; fog down the river, where it rolls defiled among the tiers of shipping, and the water-side pollutions of a great and dirty city. Fog on the Essex Marshes, fog on the Kentish Heights. Fog creeping into the cabooses of collier brigs; fog lying out on the yards, and hovering in the rigging of great ships; fog drooping on the gunwales of barges and small boats," etc., etc.

Gabriel Conroy opens as follows:

"Snow everywhere as far as the eye could reach—fifty miles looking southward from the highest peak—filling ravines and gulches, and dropping from the walls of cañons in white, shroud-like drifts, fashioning the dividing line into the likeness of a monstrous grave, hiding the bases of giant pines, completely covering young trees and larches, rimming with porcelain the bowl-like edges of still, cold lakes, undulating in motionless white billows to the edge of the distant horizon. Snow everywhere over the California Sierras on the 15th of March, 1884, and still falling."

The travelling earthquake and all the stage machinery of romantic melodrama, which Mr. Harte brings into action in *Gabriel Conroy* point, however, not to Dickens, but rather to Eugène Sue's *Wandering Jew*. The ancestry of his noble villains, the magnanimous gamblers with seraphic tenor voices, the chivalrous murderers, the generous strumpets, may be traced to that high-priest of romanticism, Victor Hugo, who delighted in the same sort of violent antitheses, defying probability and straining our credulity beyond endurance. The general attitude towards life, however lawless, exhibited in his early California tales, his disposition to find virtue in the vicious, to exalt the lowly at the expense, perhaps, of those who regard themselves as their superiors, shows the direct influence of the author of *Bleak House* and *The Christmas Carols*.

But Harte is, to my mind, the last American novelist of any eminence who can be classed as a romanticist. All our contemporary authors, with a few notable exceptions, such as Marion Crawford and Amélie Rives Chanler, deal frankly and honestly with American life, as they know it and see it; and though there are varying degrees in their power to grasp and vividly present what they see, I cannot think of one who does not aim to chronicle the particular phases of American life with which he is most intimately acquainted. While Mr. W. D. Howells (who in point of rank is *facile princeps*) preached his entertaining gospel of realism in the " Editor's Study " of *Harper's Monthly*, the critics (who as a rule are far behind the time) railed at him and professed to regard his postulate, that the novelist had to be true to the logic of life, as a piece of amusing eccentricity. He was, in their opinion, merely trying to justify his own practice. But in spite of all ridicule this proposition has, outside of England, come to be pretty generally accepted; and though the witty and genial Andrew Lang and that brilliant antediluvian, Robert Louis Stevenson, may be terribly shocked at his disrespect for Walter Scott, Mr. Howells has a valuable ally in what is called the spirit of the age, and he is bound in the end to prevail. For, as P. G. Hamerton happily puts it:

"The important service it [literature] renders to mankind is the *perpetual registering of the experiences of the race*. . . . Without a literature to record it, the experiences of dead generations could never be fully available for the living one."

Whether the majority of our contemporary novelists would subscribe to this view of their calling I do not know; but, whether they would or not, their practice sustains it. If we have an American Haggard or an American Stevenson among us, where is he? and what rank does he hold within the guild of letters? I am aware that Mr. Julian Hawthorne some years ago, entered into partnership with Inspector Byrnes and wrote some grewsome detective stories in the style of Gaboriau; and I have also seen recent tales of his in the *New York Ledger* which in blood-curdling horror rivalled *The Strange Case of Dr. Jekyl and Mr. Hyde.* But I cannot be persuaded to believe that either he or any one else regards them as serious contributions to literature. I do not question that Mr. Hawthorne is by conviction, as by inheritance, a romanticist; but there is a wide distance between the romanticism of *Bressant*, and *Beatrix Randolph* and that of *A Tragic Mystery* and *Section 558, or the Fatal Letter.*

If besides the versatile Amélie Rives we have another adherent of the defunct school among us, it is probably Mr. Harry Harland (Sydney Luska), whose first books, *As it is Written* and *Mrs. Peixada*, certainly dealt with abnormal and exceptional phases of life, and sometimes made heavy drafts upon our credulity. But if we are to judge from Mr. Harland's later works, he is rapidly shedding his romantic plumage and assuming his permanent colors among the serious chroniclers of contemporary life and manners. At all events, one will have to look very far for a more delightful bit of realism than *The Land of Love* (a study of life in the Latin Quarter in Paris); and as regards *Grandison Mather*, depicting the struggles of a young man of letters and his wife in New York, it is only less charming, but not less realistic. I have been told by those who are anxious to acquit a novelist of the charge of fidelity (they usually say " sordid fidelity ") to the humdrum prose of life that Mr. Edgar Fawcett is a romancer. In order to convince myself on this point, and correct previous impressions which might prove to be erroneous, I recently re-read three or four of Mr. Fawcett's books; and I must confess that if he is to be judged by his best, I am not for a moment in doubt as to where he properly belongs. In his admirable novel, *An Ambitious Woman*, he has given a picture of New York life which in delicate veracity and vividness is as yet unsurpassed. Mr. Fawcett knows his New York (both its upper and its nether side) as does no other American novelist, unless it be Mr. H. C. Bunner; and if it were not for the breathless haste he displays in his prolific productivity he could scarcely fail to be recognized as the brilliant and faithful chronicler of metropolitan manners that he undoubtedly is. Take such a book as *The Evil That Men Do*, which no one can read without being impressed with the enormous amount of accurate local knowledge which it implies. I take it to be no mean achievement to have painted in such striking colors the physiognomy of lower New York—the Bowery, Great Jones Street, and all the labyrinthine tangle of malodorous streets and lanes, inhabited by the tribes of Israel, the swarthy Italian, the wily Chinaman, and all the other alien hordes from all the corners of the earth. The man who can do this, and whose impulse leads him to explore with so minute an interest that *terra incognita* of polite fiction, is, whatever his friends may say to the contrary, a realist. Let them judge him by *Rutherford* and *Salarion*. I shall still persist in judging him by *An Ambitious Woman* and *The Evil That Men Do*.

To Mr. Howells more than to any one else are we indebted for the ultimate triumph of realism in American fiction. For that realism has triumphed or is triumphing no one will seriously deny who has kept track of American literature during the last quarter of a century. I do not mean by realism, of course, merely the practice of that extreme wing of the school which believes only that to be true which is disagreeable, and conscientiously omits all cheerful phenomena. Nor do I confine my definition to that minute insistence upon wearisome detail which, ignoring the relation of artistic values, fancies that a mere agglomeration of incontestable facts constitutes a truthful picture. Broadly speaking, a realist is a writer who adheres strictly to the logic of reality, as he sees it; who, aiming to portray the manners of his time, deals by preference with the normal rather than the exceptional phases of life, and, to use Henry James's felicitous phrase, arouses not the pleasure of surprise, but that of recognition. I would, therefore, include in my pantheon of realists George Eliot, Thackeray, Anthony Trollope, and Thomas Hardy; while I exclude Dickens, Wilkie Collins, Stevenson, and Haggard. I am aware that I am not in full agreement with Mr. Howells in this classification. In his recent book, *Criticism and Fiction*, he is disposed to draw the lines rather more narrowly. He puts not only Walter Scott and Dickens, but the genial biographer of Pendennis and Becky Sharp, into the outer darkness. It is, therefore, conceivable that he might also disagree with my classification of American authors, and label not only Marion Crawford and Amélie Rives, but G. W. Cable, Harold Frederic, and the late admirable Miss Woolson, with the opprobrious epithet "romantic." My space does not permit me to defend them here, but only to remark that they all have chronicled certain phases of American life with a brilliancy, delicacy, and truthfulness which no one will question. I admit that both Frederic and Miss Woolson have a lingering romantic strain which displays itself in fondness for murders; but their treatment of these sensational incidents is as realistic as that of Inspector Byrnes (in his official, not in his literary capacity). Murder in *Anne* is somehow divested of its sensational character by this insistence upon verisimilitude, which compels our credulity to keep pace with the author's invention.

Mr. Frederic has in *Seth's Brother's Wife* made the same concession to romanticism in a novel which, to those who know rural New York, is charged from beginning to end with an authenticity which enforces belief. This book, as well as *The Lawton Girl* (the scene of which is also a rural town in Central New York), has a closeness of texture and convincing quality hinting at ample stores of experience.

And this brings me to the main point of my argument. Nothing could testify with more force to the fact that we have outgrown romanticism than this almost unanimous desire, on the part of our authors, to chronicle the widely divergent phases of our American civilization. There are scarcely a dozen conspicuous

States now which have not their own local novelist. Howells, T. B. Aldrich, Miss Jewett, and Miss Wilkins have described with the pictorial minuteness and delicacy of a Meissonier the life of New England in village, city, and country. New York follows not far behind with Julien Gordon, the vivid chronicler of our fashionable life, Frederic, Fawcett, W. H. Bishop (the author of *The Home of a Merchant Prince*), H. C. Bunner, Miss Woolson, and a dozen of minor lights. Creole Louisiana has found a most faithful and delightfully artistic biographer in G. W. Cable. Virginia boasts Thomas Nelson Page, Constance Cary Harrison, and I might add Amélie Rives Chanler, if it were not for the fact that her stories might just as well be located in the moon.

Georgia's biographer, than whom I know few with a vivider touch and a more masterly grasp of character, is Richard Malcolm Johnston, the author of the delightful *Dukesborough Tales*. Tennessee has suddenly raised her head among her sister States as an aspirant for literary glory since Miss Murfree (Charles Egbert

Craddock) published her beautiful collection of tales, *In the Tennessee Mountains*. Through these and *The Despot of Broomsedge Cove*, *In the Clouds*, and *Where the Battle was Fought*, we have acquired a realizing sense of the distinctness of physiognomy which the neighbor of Kentucky presents to the world. What was hitherto a mere geographical conception, made up of some rather arbitrary lines on the map, has, through Miss Murfree's art, become an individuality, with a living countenance. For so great a service she surely deserves a monument. Of the throng of brilliant writers who have raised California to the pinnacle of a world-wide (though not quite enviable) renown, I have already mentioned Bret Harte; and Mark Twain, whose *Life on the Mississippi* and *Roughing It*, in spite of their occasional grotesqueness, are important documents of social history, has furnished the comic counterpart to Bret Harte's heroics. There are fully a dozen more who have followed in their wake; and only their number prevents me from mentioning them.

Pennsylvania and the Middle States

have, so far, lagged behind in the literary movement, and are still awaiting their authentic biographers. If Edward Eggleston had not abandoned Indiana, after his promising début with his *Hoosier Schoolmaster*, *Roxy*, etc., he might have claimed the same identification with her name as Cable and R. H. Johnston with their respective States. But in his latest novel, *The Faith Doctor*, he has moved to New York, and left James Whitcomb Riley in full possession. For Riley is a Hoosier to the backbone; and though he is primarily a poet, he possesses, in prose as in verse, the vitalizing touch of genius, which stamps everything that he produces with a vivid individuality. Illinois,* as far as I know, has as yet no novelist who is peculiarly her own; and Ohio, Kansas, and all the stripling States that stretch away to the Pacific have perhaps failed to display as yet a sufficiently distinct type to have need of a biographer. For all that, a

---

* Since the above was written a promising Illinois novelist, of realistic tendencies, has appeared in the person of Henry B. Fuller of Chicago, the author of *The Cliff-Dwellers.*

"prairie State" furnished the scene of that remarkable novel, *The Story of a Country Town*, by E. W. Howe; and Hamlin Garland (the most vigorous realist in America) has caught the very soul of that youthful virgin, Dakota, and held up to her a mirror of most uncompromising veracity.

The "Philadelphia flavor," which I am told is something very fine and very distinct, has hitherto scorned to put itself on record in literature; but recently Mr. Thomas Janvier captured it, as it were, on the wing, and wafted it into the nostrils of an expectant and appreciative world. Mr. Janvier possesses the distinction of being, up to date, the only American novelist who can boast such an achievement; though I seem to remember that a thin ghost of Philadelphia pervaded a short story which appeared in the *Century*, many years ago, by Miss Sprague, the author of *An Earnest Trifler*. I am also aware that the late Bayard Taylor was a Pennsylvanian, and that he wrote several novels (*Hannah Thurston, The Story of Kennett*, etc.), descriptive of the life of his native State; but he forsook his career as a novelist at too early a date to accomplish the task which once must have attracted him, and for which he had a most admirable equipment. His ballads "Jane Reed" and "The Old Pennsylvania Farmer" show what an exquisitely sympathetic biographer the Quaker lost in him.

It is because the American novel has chosen to abandon "the spirit of romance," which never was indigenous on this continent, and devoted itself to the serious task of studying and chronicling our own social conditions, that it is to-day commanding the attention of the civilized world. It is because Realism has ousted or is ousting Romanticism from all its strongholds that we have a literature worthy of serious consideration, and growing every year more virile, independent, and significant.

1892

THE HERO IN FICTION

SOMETIMES a nightmarish sensation comes over me that I am living somebody else's life—that I am repeating with a helpless, hideous regularity the thoughts and deeds, the blunders and successes, of some creature that lived ages ago. If heroes of fiction were endowed with the power of sensation, they would, no doubt, be oppressed with a similar consciousness of pre-existence. For most of them have not only their prototypes, but their exact counterparts, in the ages of the past. Environments may change, and are continually changing; and a certain modification in the hero's external guise and speech and sentiment may be the result of what we call "modern improvement." But in their innermost core the characters remain essentially the same. The fundamental traits of human nature, transmitted by inheritance from generation to generation, seem capable of but a limited degree of variation, and it would seem as if the novelists had already reached the limit.

The novel has existed, in one shape or another, from the earliest period of which history has preserved the record. By the novel I mean fictitious narrative in prose or verse; and when the art of writing was still unknown, the spoken story took the place of the written. Bards, rhapsodists, scalds, troubadours, ballad-singers, *improvisatori* have at different times ministered, and, in part, do yet minister, to this innate craving for fiction among the classes which are never reached by literature in the stricter sense. Whether there have been found cuneiform novels on the sun-baked bricks of Babylon and Nineveh I do not know; but the fragments of mythological poems which have been discovered suffice to show that the cuneiform equivalent for a novelist was not wanting. As for the Egyptians, their ingeniously elaborate style of writing must have been a sad restraint upon the hieroglyphic novelist when he was inclined to be prolific; and that may be one of the reasons why no hieroglyphic novels have been unearthed in tombs or temples or pyramids. The king had apparently (if we may judge by the extravagant fictions concerning himself and his deeds which he inscribed upon the public monuments) a monopoly on novel-writing, as on everything else that was pleasant and profitable. The priests worked out his plots in prose and verse, and supplied heroic embellishments *ad libitum*.

Having established this broad definition of fiction, let us take a look at the gallery of popular heroes which the novels of all ages supply. The oldest hero, as well as the newest (if we except the very latest development), is the man who looms a head above all the people. It is the king, the chieftain, the demi-god whose strength and prowess and beauty, physical or moral, thrill the soul, and kindle, by admiring sympathy, the heroic possibilities in our own hearts. Each nation sees its own ideal in this type, and modifies it in accordance with its character. Achilles, though swift-footed, brave, and beautiful, is petulant as a child, hot-tempered, and by no means a model of virtue; but, for all that, superb adjectives are heaped upon him, showing that he was meant to be a national ideal. Still nearer to this distinction comes the wily Ulysses, whose readiness of resource, faithlessness, and cheerful mendacity are so remote from Germanic notions of heroism that a modern novelist, if he used him at all, would be compelled to assign to him the part of the villain.

Siegfried, in the "Nibelungen Lied," is, perhaps, the completest general embodiment of the Germanic hero. Siegfried is, like Achilles, brave, beautiful, and strong, and he is also repeatedly described as swift (*der snelle recke*); but here the resemblance ceases. Even though the story, in the mediæval German version, may contradict the poet, when he calls him faithful, it is obvious that the potion of oblivion (which the Icelandic version supplies) is responsible for his breach of faith to Brunhild. He is truthful, gentle, forgiving, an ardent, chivalrous lover, and a chaste and affectionate husband. He resembles in many respects the Celtic King Arthur—also a god-descended hero—but is more warmly human, and less of a faultless prig. In the Icelandic version in the Elder Edda, he is wilder, more ferocious, more frankly barbarian. There is a freshness of dawn and a new-born world upon his love for Brunhild—a feature which is most exquisitely preserved in Wagner's opera "Siegfried"—but, beyond a proud truthfulness and regard for his promise, he is not troubled with many modern virtues. As an heroic type, he recurs with slight modifications in a number of the Norse sagas; and he has been and is the hero of innumerable English, German, and Scandinavian novels. In fact, the romantic school of fiction knows scarcely any other style of hero; and is forced, in order to excite admiration, to repeat the Siegfried type, more or less disguised, *ad infinitum*. Take the heroes of Walter Scott's novels, one by one (conspicuously *Ivanhoe*), and what are they but pale reflections of the general Germanic ideal? Tremendously brave, surpassingly strong, extravagantly virtuous, pursued by hostile powers which threaten to overwhelm them, but over which they ultimately triumph—is not that a fair description of the usual hero of romanticism? Whether he wears doublet and hose, or frock-coat and trousers, he is always the same fellow at heart, and he rarely fails to win, as the prize of his valor, his female counterpart, for whose sake he breaks many a lance in life's perilous tourney. In Mr. Marion Crawford's novels, *Mr. Isaacs* and *Dr. Claudius*, I recently renewed my acquaintance with the Siegfried type in a modernized guise, and in Cooper's "Leather-stocking Tales" he is perpetually recurring.

Another type of the romantic hero is represented by the fairy tale of the Poor Boy who kills the Ogre and gets the beautiful Princess and half the kingdom. Boots he used to be called in the English fairy-tale, and in the Norwegian he is called Ashiepattle. In the so-called Romantic sagas of the twelfth and thir-

teenth centuries he is a favorite hero.
He is of lowly origin, has had no advantages of education, is often buffeted and maltreated by his associates; but by dint of indomitable energy and perseverance conquers all obstacles, and finally marries his employer's daughter, or whoever else the Princess may be upon whom he has set his heart. Of course, if the author is a cruel wretch, with no regard for tender readers, he may vary the *dénouement* by landing the fair lady in the arms of the rich and hateful rival, whom the odious parent has selected for a son-in-law; but then the chances are that son-in-law No. 1 will be short-lived, and the loving hearts will be united in the last chapter. Dickens is very fond of this Ashiepattle style of hero, and has used him with success in *Dombey and Son, David Copperfield*, and many other romances. In the French novel he is the young man from the provinces who comes to Paris in *sabots*, and rises to fame and fortune. Daudet has him in *Le Nabab*, but though he gets his Princess, he has to content himself without half the kingdom. In

fact, the modern novelists, since the death of Dumas *père*, are no longer so lavish of kingdoms, and sometimes, from sheer malice, pursue Ashiepattle and his Princess beyond the honeymoon, and broadly hint that they did not "live happily ever afterwards." But that is so reprehensible that I wish it could be forbidden by an act of Congress, or that a tax might be levied (it is such an easy thing to get a tax levied, and so hard to get one removed) on every novel that does not end happily.

In the American novel, the Ashiepattle hero is very popular under the guise of the self-made man. Our national history is really a romance of the Ashiepattle among the nations, who beat the British ogre, and wedded the beautiful Princess Liberty, and conquered a kingdom compared with which those of the ancient fairy tales were scarcely worth considering. We have, therefore, a national sympathy with Ashiepattle in his struggles, and demand that his success shall be brilliant and pronounced. It will not do to cheat him out of the fruit of his labor, as Howells has done in *The Minister's Charge*, and James in *The American;* or to develop weaknesses in him which make him unworthy of success, as the former has done in *A Modern Instance*, and the latter in *Roderick Hudson*. Hardly more commendable is the example of Mr. E. W. Howe, who, in his powerful novel, *The Story of a Country Town*, made the road to success so gloomy and the success itself so modest as not to seem worth the trouble of the pursuit. It is our national comedy, as well as the national tragedy—this struggle of the Poor Boy for the Princess and half the kingdom; and we may be pardoned if we take a more personal interest in the fortunes of the hero than is compatible with artistic impartiality.

A type of hero which is happily rare in American fiction is what Rousseau calls "the grand and virtuous criminal," whom Bulwer domesticated in English literature in *Eugene Aram*. The type was popular in Germany at a much earlier period, as Schiller had invested it with the charm of his genius in Karl Moor, in

The Robbers, and in *Fiesco*. The man who wages war single-handed against a corrupt and pusillanimous society—who is forced into the career of a criminal because all roads of honorable utility are closed to him—was a direct outgrowth of the sentimental philosophy of Rousseau, and at different times occupied the fancy of every poet and novelist who came under his influence. The Problematic Character, which Goethe sketched and Spielhagen elaborately studied, is essentially the same type, and has yet an enormous vogue in the German novel. In Spielhagen, the Problematic Character ends his life on the barricades or by suicide, but usually escapes the ignominy of a jail. He is a radical of an extreme type, and labors for the reconstruction of society according to the socialistic ideal.

It will be observed that all the heroes I have so far described have one thing in common. They are all heroic. They loom a head above all the people. The heroic criminal is no exception, for he is meant to demonstrate, not his own depravity, but that of the mediocre herd

who are incapable of appreciating his
grandeur. The latest development of the
novel breaks with this tradition. It really
abolishes the hero. It has, to be sure, a
central character about whom the events
group themselves; but this central character founds his claim upon the reader's
interest, not upon any exceptional brilliancy or attraction, but upon his typical
capacity, as representing a large class of
his fellow-men. This is the great and
radical change which the so-called realistic school of fiction has inaugurated,
and it is fraught with momentous consequences. The novel, as soon as it sets itself so serious an aim, is no longer an
irresponsible play of fancy, however brilliant, but acquires an historical importance
in relation to the age to which it belongs.
The Germans are never weary of emphasizing what they call *die kulturgeschichtliche Bedeutung des Romans;* and it represents to me the final test by which a
novelist is to be judged. Thackeray, for
instance, is, to my mind, a far greater
novelist than Dickens, because he has, to
a large extent, chronicled the manners,

speech, and sentiments of England during his own day. He dealt chiefly with what is called good society, and the completeness, the truthfulness, and the vividness of his picture no one can question. Dickens, though perhaps more brilliantly equipped, had no ambition to be truthful. He had the romantic ideal in view, and produced a series of extremely entertaining tales, which are incidentally descriptive of manners, but caricatured, extravagant, and fantastic. The future historian, who should undertake to reconstruct the Victorian England from the romances of Dickens, would be justified in the conclusion that the majority of Englishmen during that period were afflicted with some cerebral disorder. He might with equal profit study *Alice Behind the Looking-Glass.*

Thackeray's heroes, then, derive their chief value from the fact of their not being heroic. Arthur Pendennis, Clive Newcome, Harry Esmond, Captain Dobbin, Rawdon Crawley, and all the rest of them,—how well we know them! How near they are to our hearts! There is a chapter of social history bound up in every one of them. They were in the best sense representative and typical. That was the way Englishmen acted, spoke, and felt during the first half of the nineteenth century. Thackeray's novels are historical documents of unimpeachable veracity. But take the Guppys, Smallweeds, Tootses, Murdocks, Betsy Trotwoods, and Micawbers—how utterly absurd and unreal they seem by comparison! A critic would have to be preternaturally acute to find in them any trace of representative value. Even George Eliot's heroes, though they are psychologically true, have less of the earthy flavor of reality about them than those of Thackeray. They were drawn, primarily, to illustrate a moral law or problem, and they are admirably adapted for this purpose. We know them; but we know them less intimately than we do Colonel Newcome and Clive and Pen. Lydgate is typical, both as to character and fate, and so are Rosamond, Casaubon, Dorothea, Gwendolen, Grandcourt, and Maggie Tulliver. But they lack the last touch of substantiality which distinguishes such a character as, for instance, old Major Pendennis or the sportive Harry Foker. They would, for the purposes of my hypothetical historian, be less valuable than the very sordid company who are immortalized between the covers of *Vanity Fair*.

Any observant reader will have noticed, as a further evidence of the evolution of fiction, that the hero of the modern novel is no longer a gentleman of leisure, whose sole business in life is to make love and run into debt. It was supposed formerly that a hero would have to be high-born, handsome, and rich in order to command the interest of young ladies (who, at all times, have been the novelist's chief patrons); and all gifts of nature and fortune were, therefore, lavished upon him. But either the sentiments of the fair damsels must have been misunderstood, or less regard is now paid to them. For the heroes of the most modern tales are apt to be men who are neither high-born nor rich; who have much business of a practical sort to attend to, and write their *billets doux* on half-sheets with the printed letter-heads of their firm. Engineers have especially developed an extraordinary popularity, in witness of which I might cite Ohnet's *Maître des Forges*, Daudet's *Jack*, Mrs. Hodgson Burnett's *That Lass o' Lowrie's*, and a multitude of others. The merchant, the editor, the farmer, and even the reporter and the clerk and the farm-hand are now attracting the attention of the novelist, and they are being portrayed not only in their leisure hours, but in their offices among bills of exchange and boxes, bales and barrels, ploughs and harrows. "The novelist," says the German critic, Julian Schmidt, "must seek the German people where the German people is to be found, *i. e.*, at its labor." And it is not only the German people which is to be found at its labor. In France Zola has, in the Rougon-Macquart series, chronicled both the legitimate and the illegitimate trades, and conscientiously outraged all heroic traditions. The American people has probably less leisure than any nation under the sun, and its novelists, if they aim at realism, must acquire the art of converting the national industries into literary material. Mr. Howells has made an admirable experiment in this direction in *The Rise of Silas Lapham*, which depicts a typical American merchant, a self-made man, in his strength as in his limitations. We see the whole life of the man in all its important phases; his pride in his mineral paint; his social insecurity and awkwardness; his pleasure in his horses; his relations with his family. In short, Colonel Silas Lapham is as vivid a reality to us as any of his counterparts around the corner, whom we meet daily, but do not know half so well. Silas Lapham, however, enables us to know them better and to judge them more justly.

I am aware that journalists are disposed to resent the picture which Mr. Howells has drawn of them in Bartley Hubbard, in *A Modern Instance*. It is, perhaps, possible that Bartley is not strikingly typical as a journalist; but that he embodies a very prevalent type in our national life is, I think, beyond dispute.

The unscrupulous smart young man, with a kind of superficial cleverness, but utterly destitute of moral sense—who is there among us who does not know him to his cost? There is not an American village which cannot exhibit him in numerously varied editions. I believe that it is also a fact that he is apt to drift into journalism, as offering the shortest and easiest road to the eminence which he feels sure is within his reach.

There is not another American novelist who has apprehended so deeply and portrayed so faithfully two such types of our national life as Silas Lapham and Bartley Hubbard. Mr. James does not know the country well enough to achieve anything so vital in the way of American portraiture, and each new book which he puts forth shows a further alienation from his nationality. His point of view is already that of the American colonist in Paris, London, or Rome, who has learned to apologize for his origin. Even such types as Mr. Newman in *The American*, and Roderick and Rowland in *Roderick Hudson* (admirable though they be), lack the strong flavor of the soil which delights us in Bartley and Silas. While Mr. Howells appears to be getting a stronger grip on reality, as it fashions itself on this side of the Atlantic, Mr. James soars, like a high-bred and cynical eagle, in the upper air of the best British society, and looks down upon his former country with a sad, critical disapproval. Nevertheless, these two novelists, each within his own sphere and limitations, represent the latest evolution of realistic fiction. Their unheroic heroes are, as a rule, social types; and if (as I devoutly hope) long lives and unimpaired vigor be granted them, they may leave behind them a national portrait-gallery which will repay the study of the future historian.

1889

AMERICAN LITERARY CRITICISM

IFTEEN years ago, during a visit to Paris, I had the pleasure of spending an evening at the house of Alphonse Daudet. There were half a dozen gentlemen present, nearly all of them bearers of distinguished names. An editor of a literary periodical who was among the guests was good-humoredly taken to task by a young author for the capriciousness, the absence of principle, in the criticisms he admitted to his journal.

"Well," he asked, "can you define to me the right principle of criticism?"

"I can," ejaculated a vivacious novelist (though not the one addressed).

"Let us have it."

"'Une main lave l'autre.
  Lavez la mienne, et je laverai la vôtre.'"

A Homeric laugh greeted this sally; but in the discussion that followed it was conceded that it was not at all amiss. It described the principle openly, though not avowedly, practised. The editor, though he made no specific admission, treated the matter jocosely, and thereby demonstrated that he did not regard the charge as a very serious one.

I have frequently, in later years, been reminded of the above couplet, when reading the criticisms of books in the daily press. The hand that has been washed or is expecting to be washed is often glaringly visible. If it is not the writer's, it is apt to be the editor's or the proprietor's; or that of the latter's interest as embodied in the counting-room. The attention which in nine journals out of ten is paid to a publication does not depend primarily upon its intellectual or æsthetic value, but upon the publisher's relations to the journal, and the amount of advertising which he is able to dispense. I do not contend, of course, that there is anything deeply reprehensible in this. For under the purely commercial view of journalism which in the last decade has become well-nigh universal, a newspaper is scarcely to be blamed for making the most advantageous use of its space, compatible with the general principles of morality and decency. The mere favor bestowed upon or withheld from an author, for reasons which have nothing to do with literature, is a venial offence, compared to the hideous and debasing sensationalism which daily empties a sewer of moral filth upon the subscriber's breakfast-table. As it is not often that a newspaper makes a feature of literary criticism, the influence which it exerts upon an author's fate is difficult to compute, but in ninety cases out of every hundred, may be put down as a vanishing quantity; while its influence upon the public, whose vision of life is largely affected by its daily résumé of the world's doings, is a very appreciable quantity, and a matter of common concern.

An author who has anything definite to say does not sit and squint at his public, while writing; nor does he trouble himself much about the opinion of the press.

The value of a criticism depends primarily upon the insight and the intellectual equipment of its author; and where these are slight, or altogether lacking, the power of the verdict for good or for ill is correspondingly small. What, for instance, can it matter to me if an anonymous young gentleman, who incidentally confesses to a warm admiration for Rider Haggard, and regards Walter Scott as the grand master of fiction—what can it matter to me, I say, if such a man finds me dull and commonplace? I have never suspended my heroines over the brinks of yawning chasms; nor have I introduced monkeys falling in love with men or men with monkeys; nor am I equal to the depicting of the perennial charms of women two thousand years old. The laurels of romancers who revel in this style of juvenile entertainment never disturb my slumbers; and the opinions of critics who take pleasure in such rubbish may amuse me, but influence me no more than the chorus of mosquitoes that hum about my ears of a summer's night. If, on the other hand, a reviewer, whether anonymous or not, shows himself to be in tolerable sympathy with my aim and my conception of what fiction should be, I read what he has to say, with a critical reservation perhaps, but yet with interest and a desire to profit by his advice. It is always a matter of some concern how your work affects an unprejudiced mind, which approaches it without friendly or hostile bias. And I may as well confess that a cordial and sympathetic review which intelligently seizes your thought and from a kindred point of view develops your merits and shortcomings, is often a source of deep gratification. Praise, unless it is discriminating, and shows maturity of judgment, has none other than a commercial value; and I sometimes even question if it has that.

A consensus of silence would, no doubt, in the case of an unknown author, kill his book; and would, even in the case of a famous one, prove highly injurious; but (if the opinion of the trade is to be trusted) vociferous and elaborate abuse is, for commercial purposes, scarcely less valuable than praise. It is the amount of attention which a work arouses that, generally speaking, determines its fate. And yet while I am writing this, half a dozen exceptions occur to me which seem to disprove the rule. The late Rev. E. P. Roe never attracted much attention from the newspapers (and the more authoritative journals ignored him altogether); and yet he rejoiced in a popularity which threw all his competitors into the shade. I remember he once showed me some scant paragraphs ridiculing one of his books; and he asked me if I could suggest any explanation of the hostile attitude of the press toward him. I offered a rather lame one, being unwilling to hurt his feelings; for he was a lovable man, of a singularly sweet nature, and the very best of friends. "The fact is," he said, "I can't discover that the newspapers affect the sale of a book one way or another. The people whom I reach read very few newspapers; and I think they are more influenced by their neighbors' opinions than by anything they read."

"What then, in your judgment, determines the success of a book?" I asked.

"Well, I should say its nearness to the life and thought of average men and women," Mr. Roe replied.

"How do you mean?"

"I mean that what the critics call art removes the book from the intelligence of ordinary people. I have been blamed because there is not art enough in my novels. Well, to be frank, there is as much art in them as there is in me. No more and no less. I never try to write down to any one's intelligence; but I write as well as I am able to write, and then let the art take care of itself. No one could have been more surprised than I was at the great success of my first books, unless it were the newspapers; but my explanation is that I happen to feel and think very much as the average plain American feels and thinks, and my manner of expressing myself is such as he, without effort, can understand. When a man does his best, he can afford to ignore the critics."

The above conversation, which took place during a drive in the neighborhood of Cornwall-on-the-Hudson, lingered long in my memory, because it strongly reinforced an opinion expressed a few years earlier by Dr. J. G. Holland, who enjoyed for a score of years a popularity of the same order and magnitude as Mr. Roe. Dr. Holland, however, took the contemptuous treatment of the critics much more to heart than Mr. Roe apparently did; and the epithet, "the American Tupper" (invented, if I remember rightly, by the New York *Sun*), rankled in his gentle mind. Even though the sale of his books ran up into hundreds of thousands, the tolerant patronage or undisguised sneer of the reviewer remained the drop of gall in the cup of his happiness.

I remember once discussing Dr. Holland's popularity with Bayard Taylor, who was at that time literary editor of the *Tribune* and the most prominent member of the guild of newspaper critics. He professed to regard it as a most mysterious phenomenon; and maintained that popularity and fame were entirely distinct things, the former being by no means a passport to the latter. Without disputing the distinction, I endeavored to suggest a rational explanation of Dr. Holland's hold upon the American public.

"What an author gives in his books," I observed, "is primarily himself—his personality. Now Dr. Holland's personality is a noble and lovable one. I have known no man who has impressed me more strongly with his personal worth—the genuine goodness and sweetness of his character—than Dr. Holland. His writing is a spontaneous pouring forth of his own soul; and the American public—the great mass whom Lincoln called the plain people—recognize the man behind the book, and feel the elevating influence which he exerts."

Taylor, with his German culture and his detestation of the narrow New England Presbyterianism, whose incorporation he saw in Dr. Holland, had no toleration for such a view, maintaining, justly enough, that some of the greatest literary artists had been pretty bad characters; and that it was intellect and the artistic sense, not morality, which entitled a man to a place in the world of letters.

I called attention, in my turn, to his distinction between popularity and fame, and reaffirmed my opinion that character frequently counts for more in the former, as intellect surely does in the latter. And it was not to be deplored that men like Dr. Holland who exerted so great a power for good were the favorites of the American public.

Bayard Taylor, though naturally sanguine, had, as the above conversation indicates, in his later years slight confidence in the public at large, and still less in his colleagues of the press. It always exasperated him to be referred to (in reviews of his poetical works) as "the great American traveller;" and he felt perpetually handicapped in his later and more serious activity by his early popularity as a writer of books of travel. "My case," he said, "is like that of a sculptor who, on account of poverty, was obliged to make his start in life as a bricklayer. When he had gained the means to supplement his deficient culture, he began to model in clay and make statues in marble.... Now, if this sculptor shows himself a worthy member of the artistic guild and produces work of artistic merit, is it fair to be forever saying to him: 'You were such an excellent bricklayer. Why didn't you continue to lay bricks?' That is exactly what the American public is continually saying to me. I haven't a particle of pride in my books of travel, . . . and if I have no other title to remembrance, I shall be content to be forgotten."

When, a few months before his death, he had finished his lyrical drama, "Prince Deukalion," he said to me:

"This poem of mine will, I fear, not mean much to the average American, who would like to run as he reads. I am aware that it will appeal only to the few, who have thought somewhat on the same lines as myself. I shudder to think what the newspaper critic will make of it. Therefore I am going to ask you to do me a favor. Will you write a review of the poem from the advance sheets I sent you—for *Scribner's Monthly?* Stedman has offered to review the book in the *Atlantic*, and McDonough in the *Tribune*. Now let it be fully understood that I don't want you to feel under any obligation to praise. I know that you understand the poem; and I only want you to strike the key-note, as it were, for its interpretation. It is nonsense to say (as many, no doubt, will say) that, if it is worth anything, it will be understood by the average reader without any commentary. For this once, I am anxious to be completely and sympathetically understood. I have never made the least effort to secure a favorable hearing for anything I have written; and I want you to promise, as far as possible, to eliminate your friendly feeling for me. It is not your friendship I need, but your intelligence."

I wrote the review, as desired, after having acquainted Dr. Holland with the author's wishes; but before the February number of *Scribner's Monthly* (1879) reached Berlin, Bayard Taylor was dead.

To me, his anxiety to be understood, and the precaution he took to secure intelligent comment upon his work, though, perhaps, a reflection upon the newspaper critic, were not only natural, but commendable. It was because he knew the fraternity so well, and was so thoroughly acquainted with its general intellectual equipment, that he had such serious misgivings. And yet the three men he selected to interpret his thought were all more or less closely identified with the critical guild; and though not professional journalists held semi-official relations to journalism. I was myself, at that time, semi-editorially connected with three prominent publications which were in the habit of sending me books for review; and the experiences I accumulated in this capacity, though they were not all agreeable, I would not have dispensed with for a small fortune.

The dilemma upon whose horns I was always in danger of being impaled was the endeavor to reconcile kindness and justice. I was not one of those who cherish a grudge against a man for having achieved a book; and I dare assert that I picked up every novel or poem that was sent me with a kindly fellow-feeling for the author and a desire to view him in the most favorable light. But frequently, when I had read a page or two, the reflection would obtrude itself that this was after all a very ephemeral performance; and by the time I had finished fifty pages, most of my benevolent intentions would, perhaps, be chilled, and my critical impulses would bristle like the quills upon the fretful porcupine. Had I the right to commend such feebleness—such vague and muddled thought, so clumsily expressed—for fear of hurting the author's feelings? Was I not practising an imposition on the public if I misrepresented the character of a book, and perhaps induced scores of people to buy it who otherwise would have left it alone? I came to the conclusion, after a brief wavering, that I should be doing neither the author nor his reader a kindness in uttering vapid compliments—or talking learned, laborious stuff with a view to concealing my real opinion.

I am bound to confess that none of the three journals with which I was then connected nor any of those which have later engaged my services endeavored in any way to influence my judgment. Never did I receive an editorial hint as to the tone in which I ought to review this or that book. But by a curiously indirect process I was once made to feel that I was too good-natured, and that I was in future expected to be more severe. For in two successive reviews of mine, all the complimentary portions were stricken out, and only the censure was permitted to remain. When I complained of this treatment to a friend, who had had a similar experience, he told me that I must be aware that the journal in question made a specialty of damning. Its traditional tone was one of superior condescension, or cynical forbearance. The man who praised, without some qualifying censure, could not long remain *personâ gratâ* in its editorial sanctum.

He was entirely right; and I have found since that, unless a critic has an intimate and accurate knowledge of the traditions of his paper, he will be sure to run against invisible and unsuspected snags. I know one great newspaper which invariably damns or ignores the publications of a certain publishing house, and (if the report be true) as a rule is predisposed in favor of the books of another. I give this, however, as rumor, not as incontestable fact.

If I may trust my own experience, I should say that a book stood a far better chance of being judged on its merits ten or fifteen years ago than it does now. The monthly magazines gave then a large amount of space to "Recent Literature," and they often gave the cue to the more ephemeral publications. I have never ceased to regret the disappearance of the excellent department devoted to "Culture and Progress" in the old *Scribner's Monthly* and the *Century Magazine;* and the "Open Letters" seem to me a poor and inadequate substitute. The idea that the newspaper critic (because he comes earlier) has the advantage of the magazine critic and makes him superfluous is, to my mind, a lamentable error. *Harper's Magazine* held, as long as Mr. W. D. Howells occupied its "Editor's Study," a unique position, and contained some of the subtlest, justest, and most admirably vigorous and discriminating critical writing that it ever has been my good-fortune to read. And, what was more, it was discussed in hundreds of newspapers all over the country, and produced a great and lasting effect. I do not mean to insinuate, of course, that Mr. Howells's successor, Mr. Charles Dudley Warner, is less able and brilliant; but his critical point of view is so alien to mine that, with all my admiration for his wit and his beautiful style, I am unable to do him full justice.

Even the *Atlantic Monthly*, which once exerted so great an influence as a literary censor (not to speak of the *North American Review*), has abolished its department of "Recent Literature," while yet devoting from time to time some pages in the body of the magazine to the discussion of important publications. The more credit does the *Cosmopolitan* deserve for maintaining a literary department (under the title "In the Library") which unites finish of style and a certain epigrammatical snap and sparkle with the keenest acumen and the soundest judgment. I know indeed no wielder of the critical lance in the United States, unless it be Mr. M. W. Hazeltine, of the *Sun*, who in point of scholarship, perspicacity, and hospitality of mind rivals Mr. Brander Matthews. He does not beat about him with cheap catch-words; nor does he, like so many of his colleagues, assume airs of lofty superiority and pat the poor author on the back, telling him not to be discouraged even if he fails to pass muster before such an august authority as the reviewer in question.

There is, I suppose, an evolution in literary criticism, as in all other human concerns. The process of differentiation which has eliminated the department of "Recent Literature" from most of the monthly magazines, has in this country as in England been instrumental in relegating the book review to special journals. The *Nation*, which commands a wide range of expert opinion, has long held a pre-eminent position and scalped many a rising novelist with a neatness and despatch which could not but challenge the victim's admiration. The *Critic*, which is now twelve years old and has long since vindicated its right to existence, is conducted with conspicuous ability; and the *Literary World*, of Boston, which counts nearly a score of years, furnishes also an admirably clear and comprehensive survey of the intellectual movements of the age. A younger rival, for which I confess to a considerable predilection, is the semi-monthly *Dial* of Chicago—distinguished for its broad-minded impartiality and scholarship, and a typographical beauty which gives an added zest to the perusal of its bright and instructive pages.

It is probable, however, that with the growing tendency to specialization which is characteristic of modern life, some of these weekly and bi-weekly journals, devoted solely to literary criticism, will continue to grow in authority and prosperity, until they will monopolize the field. It is obvious to every attentive reader that each of the more prominent ones is already acquiring a temperament as distinct as that of the English *Spectator* or the *Saturday Review*. They are accumulating a fine assortment of likes and dislikes (intelligent or unintelligent according to your point of view); they are attaching to themselves a large corps of experts, in the most varied fields, and are gradually attaining the importance, the individuality, and the traditions befitting permanent institutions.

1893

AMERICA IN EUROPEAN LITERATURE

HEN Æneas met Achilles in Hades, the swift-footed son of Thetis, according to Virgil, was suffering from the blues. There was a certain weary monotony about the life in the nether world, he complained—a shadowy futility which made existence a burden. I remember the time when, to the cultivated classes in Europe, America presented a picture not unlike the Greek conception of Hades. Life here was supposed to be devoid of all higher pleasures, dreary, and destitute of all charm; but beyond this, the land was a shadow-land, and all ideas concerning it were hazy and indefinite. The laws of cause and effect which prevail in Europe were supposed to have no validity on this

side of the ocean; and all reasoning concerning the country and its people was therefore conceded to be unsafe. If I had told my grandmother in Norway that two and two made five in America, I do not believe it would have surprised her. She had seen what was to her a much more startling phenomenon. A slovenly, barefooted milkmaid named Guro, who had been in her employ, had returned from the United States, after an absence of five years, with all the airs of a lady, and arrayed in silks and jewelry which in Norway represented a small fortune. My grandmother was convinced that Guro (who had never been a favorite with her) had crossed the ocean for the sole purpose of dazzling her, triumphing over her, and enjoying her discomfiture. For she had prophesied Guro a bad end, and she bore a lasting grudge against the country which had brought her prophecy to naught.

These complete transformations, wrought by a transatlantic sojourn, were by no means rare occurrences in my childhood. Gawky stable-boys who never wore a coat except on Sundays returned attired in broadcloth and stove-pipe hats, which immensely impressed their countrymen. A certain vulgar impudence and dash of manner which they likewise had acquired in the far West were no less envied and admired. The country in which such things could happen could scarcely be subject to ordinary mundane laws. It presented itself to the imagination as a shadowy fable-land, where fortune might overtake a man as it did Boots in the fairy-tale; where all things were possible, except that which might have been expected.

It is but natural that these notions concerning the United States, as a sort of dreary and vulgar fable-land, emancipated from the laws of probability, should find ·their reflection in literature. The Uncle from America was long a standing character in the French and the German drama, and occasionally also invaded the novel. He was a benevolent *Deus ex machinâ*, and so enormously rich that, like Dumas's Monte Cristo, he never carried less than a million for small change in his vest pocket. By the gift of a few hundred thousands, and the promise of as many millions after his death (for the Uncle from America was always a bachelor), he put his nephew, the poor but worthy lover, in a position to triumph over all obstacles. The cruel parents relented; the dutiful daughter, whose heart had all along been his, gave him joyfully her hand; and the delightful uncle, in dispensing his blessing, in the final tableau, usually declared that he had lived but for this moment, and that it rewarded him for his life-long toil.

It was, of course, only as long as the haziest notions concerning the United States prevailed that this kind of uncle could flourish, and as a matter of fact he is not frequently met with in the contemporary drama or novel. The · last time I encountered him was in a recent novelette entitled *Monika Waldvogel*, by the German author Wilhelm Jensen. The uncle there, who is as eccentric and shrewd as he is benevolent, returns (as every good German should) to his Fatherland to enjoy his American millions, hunts up the last two representatives of his family, buys a large estate, and makes a will, in which the niece, Monika, is made sole heir, on condition that she shall offer a permanent home in her house to her remote male cousin, for whom she has a particular aversion. If, however, she marries him, the estate is to go to the residuary legatee, whose name is to be found in a sealed envelope. After a certain time, spent in the fiercest hostilities, the Amazon is conquered by Achilles, and determines to surrender the estate to the residuary legatee, who proves to be herself with the matrimonial prefix to her name. The American Uncle, who here follows the legitimate avuncular vocation, is amusingly, though not very convincingly, portrayed; but his American flavor is of the very vaguest kind. German authors, when they need that style of uncle nowadays, usually make him hail from India or Borneo or Morocco, or some such *terra incognita;* for America has, by perpetual intercourse, been made to assume a more and more definite character, and has thereby been largely spoiled for purposes of romance. In Lindau's recent novel *Mr. and Mrs. Bewer* (and a charming novel it is) the returning Crœsus comes from the far East; while his American brother (who hails from California) is only moderately rich, and the latter's American wife and sister-in-law are represented as being well-bred and warm-hearted women, and not strikingly unconventional.

It is interesting to note that since the shadowy stage has been passed an author's attitude towards the United States is determined, not so much by his knowledge of the country as by his political principles. An author with Tory proclivities (like Ouida or the late Lord Beaconsfield) is sure to cherish a more or less pronounced animosity towards the great democratic republic; and to represent it as the home of pretentious vulgarity, ridiculous snobbishness, and ignorance of all that gives a higher value to existence. Authors inclined towards radicalism, on the other hand, although they are not blind to the vulgarity of certain classes of Americans, refuse to accept these as representative; and dwell with preference on the practical ingenuity and skill of our people, their shrewd common-sense, and freedom from feudal prejudice. The young man who, because of his exceptional daring and nobility of soul, refuses to fit in anywhere in the ancient feudal machinery, and whose life would have been crushed or broken by the stubborn and complicated tangle of ancient abuses and wrongs, finds, in the radical drama or novel, promptly his place in the New World, and develops there to his full spiritual stature. It is, according to this class of writers, the humdrum, mediocre soul, which drowsily accepts whatever is, and lacks the courage to grapple with troublesome problems—it is this type of soul which thrives in the ancient society and gives it its color and character. The Philistine is so strong, not because he is brave, but because he is so numerous. Samson, though shorn of his locks, has yet strength enough left to shake the pillars of the temple; but the temple buries him in its fall. But if Samson had gone to the United States, instead of succumbing to the charms of Delilah, he could have disported himself with the jawbone of the ass to his heart's content, and nobody would have molested him. That is the impression we derive from the radical optimists who wage war in their novels and plays against the old social order, and who in their innocence believe that the ancient spirit of caste and religious hatred and prejudice have no vogue and no force in the happy Atlantic beyond the sea. In Spielhagen's novels the socialistic agitator, who wants to turn everything upside down, is usually a German who has spent a period of years in the United States, and acquired here a wholesome audacity of thought and the ability to penetrate to the bottom of all shams. In Auerbach's *Black Forest Village Tales*, "The Gawk," who has been the sport and the scapegoat of his native town, becomes a useful and respected citizen in Ohio, and writes a letter home which furnishes the illustrator of the book with the subject for a tail-piece, consisting of two luxuriant palm-trees. In fact, transformations of this kind are frequent in Auerbach; and the palm-trees from Ohio are symbolic of his realism in transatlantic affairs.

It was to be expected that the Norwegian authors, who are all pronounced liberals, would deal with the United States as a land of refuge and redemption for problematic characters. The old fossilized society has become rigid; in its anxious instinct of self-preservation it respects no one's individuality, if it differs from that of the majority, and forces every one who does differ into hypocrisy and lies. The great Norwegian dramatist, Ibsen, has made this the theme of a very effective drama called "The Pillars of Society." Consul Bernick, the hero, has during long years spun himself into a net of dissimulation and falsehood, in his endeavor to conform to the moral ideal of the society, whose "pillar" he feels himself to be. He forces his son into the same strait-jacket, regardless of the fact that the boy's wholesome individuality and natural gifts rebel against it; and the result is alienation between father and son, between husband and wife, between all who naturally belong together, simply because no one dares be himself, but must do homage to the norm of thought, speech, and conduct which society has established, and upon which it has set the seal of its approval. The *dénouement* in these painful complications is precipitated by the arrival of a very curious person— a spinster named Lona, from the United States. This Lona had loved Bernick in his youth and been loved by him; but for social reasons they had parted. Life in the United States has now freed her from all foolish prejudice, and she is, in fact, surprisingly "emancipated" from all antiquated notions of propriety and morals. I have met ladies resembling her at a Woman's Rights Convention in Boston, but I doubt if they would have been much of an acquisition to any society except the one in which I found them. Ibsen's Lona, however, is meant to be a great deal wiser and pleasanter than she is, judged by the effect she produces upon Bernick and his family. One of the characters, Martha, who has for half a lifetime waited for a lover who cannot afford

to marry, exclaims, after having heard
Lona's description of American life:
"Yes, over there it must be beautiful; a
wider sky and clouds that sail higher than
here; and a freer air blows over the people." In Björnson's novel, *The Heritage
of the Kurts*, the United States is similarly
represented, as a land that has much to
teach Europe, particularly in technical
education and pedagogics; and an American lady who is not in the least caricatured comes over to Norway in order to
impart new ideas on the subject of education. The definiteness, self-restraint, and
absence of all utopianism in this description, testify sufficiently to the fact that
Björnson has spent a year in this country and knows whereof he speaks. If he
had drawn upon his imagination for his
facts, his Massachusetts school-mistress
would, no doubt, have approximated the
type of Ibsen's Lona. In the novels of
Jonas Lie, another well-known Norwegian author, the United States likewise
figures as a land in which many a lesson
of practical wisdom can be learned; and
his returned Norse-Americans are usually

better and abler men for their sojourn beyond the sea. In his *Family at Gilje* the captain's son, who for many a weary year has struggled in vain with the uncongenial Latin and Greek, escapes from his classical sufferings to the land of liberty, and there turns out to be a mechanical genius, and gains wealth and position. It is not "genteel" in Norway to train one's self in the mechanical arts. Society prescribes but two ways to influence and position in the state—viz., the one through the military academy and the other through the university; and the father who does not wish his son to be *déclassé* compels him, regardless of his proclivities, to choose the one path or the other.

It is a curious fact that in no European literature is America more persistently misrepresented than in that of France. With the exception of Ludovic Halévy, who seems to have studied Mrs. Mackay's *salon* with a not unkindly interest, I can recall no prominent French novelist who does not burlesque American speech and manners whenever the opportunity presents itself. But then Halévy, with all his Gallic *esprit*, is a Jew, therefore scarcely representative. Édouard Laboulaye, to be sure, was conspicuous as the particular champion of our republic, and in his ingenious fable, *Paris in America*, gave a utopian picture of American life, as it was supposed to be forty years ago; but nobody took that seriously, except its author, who with charming *naïveté* prided himself on his power of poetic divination. I cannot recall any reference to the United States in Daudet; and of Zola I have not read enough to have a right to speak. In the dramas of Sardou and Dumas *fils* the references are mostly contemptuous, and the transatlantic characters who are introduced would, if they were real, amply justify their author's scorn. When, as occasionally happens, a French author is too kind-hearted or too regardful of probabilities to kill his villain at the opportune moment, he is apt to ship him to the United States. As a means of just retribution it amounts to the same thing, the one punishment being held to be no less severe than the other. Of course, I am here speaking of *belles-lettres*, for in descriptions of travel and politico-economical works, like De Tocqueville's famous *Democracy in America*, there are found many just and shrewd observations, and many betraying keenness of insight and the broadest cosmopolitan spirit.

A survey of English fiction with reference to its attitude towards "the States" I do not attempt, partly because the subject is too extensive for a short article, and partly because every reader has sufficient material at hand for an independent judgment.

1887

THE ETHICS OF ROBERT BROWNING

IN my essay entitled "The Problem of Happiness"* I made the assertion that Robert Browning "preaches frankly the rights of passion, and derides in his heroes all pusillanimous regard for duty." Now a voice comes from the East and several from the West, challenging me to explain what I mean by such an insinuation. Well, then, I will be explicit. I will, for the present, ignore Browning in the capacity in which I sincerely admire him (*i.e.*, as a poet), and deal with him in the capacity in which I do not wholly admire him—viz., as a moralist. I venture to believe that I have a certain qualification for this

* *Essays on German Literature*, pp. 129-140.

task, for Browning's books have been my constant friends and companions for well-nigh fifteen years. I have lived on a close and familiar footing with Fra Lippo Lippi, Rabbi ben Ezra, Andrea del Sarto, and, above all, with that glorious company of robust saints and sinners in "The Ring and the Book." I am quite ready to subscribe to the opinion of Robert Louis Stevenson, who (in "Virginibus Puerisque") calls this poem the noblest book of the nineteenth century, in which case, of course, I count Goethe's "Faust" as belonging to the eighteenth. But so great a work it is, that I am loath to stand sponsor to an opinion which may seem to detract from its merit. What I shall say, then, is said in no censorious spirit, but in the spirit of respectful interrogation, as a disciple may speak to his master.

As I have already said, I am inclined to regard Browning as a eudemonist. Those of his characters into which he has poured his own soul have no sort of consciousness of their obligations as members of society. With a light-hearted, freebooting propensity they start out in quest of happiness, and rarely trouble themselves to consider whose rights are violated as long as they achieve their purpose. Take, for instance, that charmingly full-blooded piece of Italian Renaissance, Fra Lippo Lippi. Where have the rights of the flesh been preached more eloquently? Where do you find such sunny paganism under the cowl of one consecrated to the service of Christ? But that is in keeping with the character, you will say; it was the very birthmark of the Renaissance. Granted. Taken by itself, it does not prove much; taken in connection with a dozen or twenty instances of the same kind, it proves what I am aiming to prove, viz., the tendency of Browning to glorify the flesh. "A Light Woman" is a more striking instance. The poet tells how he alienated the affections of his friend's mistress:

" For see—my friend goes shaking and white;
   He eyes me as a basilisk;
I have turned, it appears, his day into night,
   Eclipsing his sun's disk.

"And I did it, he thinks, as a very thief;
   Tho' I love her—that he comprehends—
One should master one's passion (love in chief),
And be loyal to one's friends.

"And she—she lies in my hand as tame
   As a pear hung basking over a wall;
Just a touch to try, and off it came.
   'Tis mine—can I let it fall?

With no mind to eat it at the worst,
   Were it thrown in the road would the case assist?
'Twas quenching a dozen blue-flies' thirst
   When I gave its stalk a twist.

"And I—what I seem to my friend, you see—
   What I soon shall seem to his love, you guess.
What I seem to myself, do you ask of me?
   No hero, I confess.

"Well, anyhow, here the story stays,
   So far, at least, as I understand;
And Robert Browning, you writer of plays,
   Here's a subject made to your hand."

It is unfair, perhaps, to assume that this poem is what it appears to be—autobiographical; although Browning has taken particular pains to identify himself with the story by affixing his sign-manual, as it were—his full name in the last verse. If the manner in which it is told proves anything—and I am inclined to think that it does—it proves that moral obligations sit lightly upon this poet. I draw this conclusion from the tone that pervades the verses, rather than from any particular verse; and I doubt if any one who reads the whole will contend that it could have been written by a moralist.

Still more to the point is the beautiful poem entitled "The Statue and the Bust," which seems to have served as a model for Bret Harte's "For the King." There the Duke and the Lady—the Bride of the Riccardi—spend their lives in vainly sighing for each other. She is married, and so is, probably, he. The passion that cried out in the hearts of both for a union was wasted, not by a severe regard for duty, but by mere dalliance, lack of courage, cowardly temporizing. Their mistake was, according to Browning, that they allowed considerations of piety, prudence, and state to interfere with the immediate fulfilment of their purpose. It were better to have sinned, he thinks, than to spend one's life pining away with unsatisfied desire. If the sin, which was in their hearts, had been consummated in act, it would have been better for both.

"'Is one day more so long to wait?
   Moreover the Duke rides past. I know
   We shall see each other, sure as fate.'

"She turned on her side and slept. Just so!
   So we resolve on a thing and sleep.
   So did the lady, ages ago."

And after having expended his regret in very trenchant and incisive verses, the poet, as if to clinch his argument, adds these unmistakable lines:

"I hear your reproach—but delay was best,
   For their end was a crime! Oh, a crime
     will do
   As well, I reply, to serve for a test,

"As a virtue, golden through and through,
   Sufficient to vindicate itself
   And prove its worth at a moment's view.

"If you choose to play—is my principle—
Let a man contend to the uttermost
For his life's set prize, be it what it will.

"The counter our lovers staked was lost
As surely as if it were lawful coin.
And the sin I impute to each frustrate ghost

"Was the unlit lamp and the ungirt loin,
Though the end in sight was a crime, I say."

Those lines: "Let a man contend to the uttermost for his life's set prize, be it what it will," might serve for a motto to nearly all that Browning has written. They have a harmless look, and might readily be accepted as a maxim of practical wisdom. But this contention to the uttermost implies in Browning a disregard of all rights that clash with your own. It is individualism carried to its extreme limit. Where the sense of duty crops out in Browning, it is frequently as a thing to be brushed aside as unworthy of serious consideration. He delights so in exhibitions of the blood-red barbaric streaks in the human soul, that, I almost fancy, virtue, duty, and all pale abstractions that pull in the opposite direction affect him (in this mood) with a certain impatience. They are less interesting, less picturesque. To be sure, he is capable of painting goodness and virtue most beautifully, as, for instance, in Pompilia, in "The Ring and the Book," and the delightful Pippa in "Pippa Passes." But how much more gorgeous is the coloring, how much more resplendent the characterization of the guilty lovers, Sebald and Ottima, than of Pippa! It is power Browning admires; power, in whatever shape it may appear. Self-abnegation, abstention, renunciation, are pale negative terms which in nowise attract him, except for the psychological curiosities which they may reveal. Natural sweetness and nobility, which are but the acting out of healthy inborn instincts, command his sympathy, but it is where long-suppressed power flares out in baleful passion that he is at his best.

By passion I do not mean only the passion of love. All exhibitions of unrestrained energy, concentrated in a moment of supreme action, are to him beautiful. Happiness—individual well-being —appears the legitimate object of human pursuit, and his heart warms towards the man or woman who, instead of sipping it in slow driblets, drains it in one swift, glorious draught. Prudential restraints seem always pitiful. The young art-student and the singing-girl in "Youth and Art," both poor as church-mice, who loved each other across the house-tops, are blamed for choking up the sweet budding passion in their hearts, and aiming instead for worldly success. He is knighted and becomes an R. A.; she marries a lord and becomes a person of consequence; but in the midst of this external success both are oppressed with a deep heart-hunger—a sense of futility in whatever they undertake :

"Each life is unfulfilled, you see ;
  It hangs still, patchy and scrappy ;
We have not sighed deep, laughed free,
  Starved, feasted, despaired—been happy.

"And nobody calls you a dunce,
  And people suppose me clever ;

This could but have happened once,
And we missed it, lost it forever."

This same sense of futility is shared by Paracelsus (in the drama of that name), not because he has sinned, but because he has failed to experience any deep joy —any real happiness. It is a common punishment with Browning (as, indeed, it is with certain stormy temperaments in reality) for having failed to make the best of life's rare golden moments.

I am tempted to quote, too, as an evidence of a tendency to moral laxity, the ingenious plea for the flesh contained in the poem, "Any Wife to Any Husband." The dying wife is bitterly conscious that her husband will not remain faithful to her memory. She foresees that he will (to use the language of Dr. Berdoe) "dissipate his soul in the love of other women; he will excuse himself by the assurance that the light loves will make no impression on the deep-set memory of the woman who is immortally his bride. He will have a Titian's Venus to desecrate his wall rather than leave it bare and cold; but the flesh-loves will not impair the soul-love."

"'Ah, but the fresher faces! Is it true,'
Thou'lt ask, 'some eyes are beautiful and new?
Some hair—how can one choose but grasp such wealth?
And if a man would press his lips to lips
Fresh as the wilding hedge-rose cup there slips
The dew-drop out of, must it be by stealth?

It cannot change the love kept still for her,
Much more than such a picture to prefer
Passing a day with to a room's bare side.
The painted form takes nothing she possessed.
Yet while the Titian's Venus lies at rest,
A man looks. Once more, what is there to chide?'"

It will be said, no doubt, that Browning does not identify himself with this argument, but gives it merely as a bit of interesting and deeply human soul-history. I cannot quite agree with this view. Upon me it makes the impression of a thing intensely felt and experienced. It has unmistakably the autobiographical note, and as such coincides perfectly with the sentiment of the poems already quoted.

As it is by the cumulative effect of my quotations that the correctness of my views is to be proved, I am inclined to impose upon the reader's patience by a few more examples. I doubt if there is one more striking to be found in all Browning than the long argument of the Pope Innocent III. in " The Ring and the Book," reviewing the alleged crime of the priest Caponsacchi in virtually eloping with another man's wife. It will be remembered that Pompilia is the wife of the fiendish Count Guido Franceschini, who murders her and her foster-parents. In accordance with the laws of the Church, the priest, even though their relation may be morally blameless, has been guilty of a crime which calls for condign punishment. But the aged Pope is filled with sympathy and admiration for the daringly generous act. This is noble language, indeed, which he employs in summing up the *pros* and *cons* of Caponsacchi's plea :

"Do I smile?
Nay, Caponsacchi; much I find amiss,
Blameworthy, punishable in this freak
Of thine, this youth prolonged though age
    was ripe,
This masquerade in sober day . . .
. . . . . let him judge,
Our adversary, who enjoys the task!
I rather chronicle the healthy rage
When the first moan broke from the mar-
    tyr maid
At that uncaging of the beasts—made bare
My athlete on the instant, gave such good,
Great, undisguised leap over post and pale
Right into the mid-cirque, free fighting
    place.
There may have been rash stripping—every
    rag
Went to the winds—infringement manifold
Of laws prescribed pudicity, I fear,
In this impulsive and prompt self-display!
. . . .
Men mulct the wiser manhood, and suspect
No veritable star swims out of cloud.
Bear thou such imputation; undergo
The penalty I nowise dare relax—
Conventional chastisement and rebuke.
But for the outcome—the brave, starry
    birth,
Conciliating earth with all that cloud—
Thank Heaven, as I do!"

And the saintly Pompilia, who loves the priest as he loves her, with a half-spiritual, half-earthly passion—does she regret having disregarded conventional morality and escaped from the cruel marriage-bond in his company? No; dying, she glories in his love:

> "I feel for what I verily find—again
> The face, again the eyes, again through all
> The heart and its immeasurable love
> Of my one friend, the only, all my own,
> Who put his breast between the spears and me.
> Ever with Caponsacchi!   .   .   .
> O lover of my life! O soldier-saint!
> No work begun shall ever pause for death.
> Love will be helpful to me more and more
> I' the coming course, the new path I must tread,
> My weak hand in thy strong hand strong for that."

The bias which I have here indicated is one that is very natural to a poetical temperament. But Browning is so multiform, so many-sided, so richly equipped, that it seems scarcely possible to emphasize one phase of his personality without, by implication, doing injustice to several correlative ones. I am far from pretending to have expounded Browning's philosophy in these detached comments. Being healthily robust in dealing with the passions, he leaves morality to take care of itself. On the other hand, no living poet has a deeper insight into the secret recesses of the soul than he; no one is more capable of putting himself *en rapport* with spiritual exaltation, ascetic enthusiasm, religious fanaticism, or of describing the mood and action of the soul upon its loftiest heights. This is the true dramatic faculty, which makes an author transmute himself into a sinner or saint, scholar or ploughman, brute or angel, as the poetic exigency demands. And this faculty no English poet since Shakespeare has possessed in so high a degree. The only thing, in my opinion, which prevents him from overshadowing all contemporaries is the needlessly obscure and crabbed language in which he often chooses to clothe his transcendent thoughts. But even admitting his unmelodiousness, and deploring the prolixity and intricate snarls of his latest verse, I yield to none in my admiration of Robert Browning. He belongs in the company of the very greatest.

1888

MARS vs. APOLLO

SOME years ago I visited the studio of a famous Berlin sculptor. He was modelling a small group representing a lieutenant who has just returned from a reconnoitring expedition, bringing some important intelligence to his superior officer. A casemate torn by a bomb, and a dozen stacked guns formed the background. It was intended to be cast in bronze as a mantel ornament, or possibly a clock. Round about the studio were similar subjects, some in plaster, and others in clay. The cannon, the rifle, the bugle, the sword — in fact, all the instruments of war—were seen wherever you turned.

" Do you, artistically speaking, regard the gun as a beautiful object?" I asked the sculptor.

"No, I regard it, artistically speaking, as a hideous object," he answered.

"But it represents to you something which you think is beautiful?" I persisted.

"Yes," he said with a chuckle; "it represents to me, in the present case, fifteen hundred marks easily earned. What can be more beautiful, unless it were fifteen thousand marks?"

"But, joking aside, would you regard me as impertinent if I ask you why you keep on modelling guns, when you think them hideous?"

"My dear sir," he replied, with a significant shrug of the shoulders, "one must live."

A few days later, when visiting an exhibition of modern paintings, I was again struck by the great prevalence of martial subjects. Mars was the deity whom these artists worshipped; it was he who led the dance of the muses on Mount Helicon, and no longer Apollo. Bloodshed and slaughter were glorified; here the chieftains of war, in shining harness, mounted upon superb steeds, were receiving the homage of the conquered neighbors beyond the Rhine; there the wounded and the dying were half raising themselves on their elbows, swinging their blood-bespattered caps, and with breaking voices cheering the Emperor and Bismarck, or the Crown Prince and Von Moltke as they rode by. It was a pitiful spectacle to see the arts thus degraded, enslaved, pressed into the service of barbarism instead of advancing and glorifying civilization.

I cannot cite all the evidence of Apollo's subjection to Mars, which accumulated on my hands during the sojourn in Germany to which I refer. Only one more observation will suffice. It was my particular business at that time to study German educational methods, and I frequently obtained permission to attend recitations in public and private schools of various grades. On one occasion I was present during the hour for declamation of poetry in one of the lowest classes of a gymnasium. A small boy of eight, with painfully thin arms and legs, and spectacles on his nose, stood up and recited in a child's shrill voice a tremendously patriotic rhyme, bristling with national braggadocio, hatred of the French, and the most blood-thirsty sentiments. That little, spectacled fellow with his deplorable spindle-shanks was snorting and panting for the blood of the Gaul, and the teacher sat at his desk and smiled approvingly at the deluded child's ferocity, which he mistook for patriotism. Presently another valiant warrior of about the same age got up and spouted with ludicrous vigor Arndt's

"Der Gott der Eisen wachsen liesz
Er wollte keine Knechte."

He was followed by three or four others, one of whom recited Körner's beautiful "Battle Prayer," and another a hyperloyal greeting to the Emperor by an obscure author.

In France the martial spirit in the arts is no less conspicuous and aggressive. There, too, the picture galleries are crowded with battle scenes; though it is the victories of the remoter past they celebrate, not the defeats and humiliations of 1870. There, too, the majority of public monuments represent great chieftains of war, and commemorate battles and martial achievements. Whether the little boys in the public schools are taught in their recitations of poetry and text-books of history to hate the Germans, and to yearn for the day of vengeance, I do not know positively, but I think it highly probable. The barbaric martial spirit, upon which princes and nobles rely for their continuance in power, is naturally encouraged by them; and the fine arts, which have the same need of bread as less exalted industries, court their favor by appearing to be imbued with their spirit. The muses and graces dance their alluring dance about the rough and brutal Mars, "striking the earth with rhythmic feet," and joining their sweet voices in a martial chorus.

It is a matter of congratulation that in this country the arts have largely emancipated themselves from the sway of Mars. Battle-pieces are comparatively rare in our Academy exhibitions, and cannon, guns, and bayonets are never introduced in ornamental bric-à-brac. To be sure, our great generals and admirals have their niches secure in the temple of fame, and their ugly statues on our public squares; and every little town East or West which sent soldiers to the War has its soldiers' monument, consisting of an obelisk inscribed with the names of the fallen, or a boy in blue leaning upon his gun. But these monuments are more in the nature of a commemoration of the individual men than a glorification of their martial calling. Our poets do not often sing of battles and carnage, though occasionally they single out heroic feats, performed in war, as subjects worthy of their muse. Thus Read has celebrated "Sheridan's Ride," in strong and spirited verse, Lathrop, "Kearney at Five Forks," and Whittier, "Barbara Frietchie." But considering the duration of the Civil War, and the many brilliant feats of arms which made it memorable, the amount of poetry which it produced was remarkably small. Among all our great poets I cannot recall a single martial spirit. Walt Whitman's "My Captain, oh my Captain," is perhaps the noblest poem of the war period, always, of course, excepting Lowell's "Commemoration Ode." But neither is written in a warlike spirit. Both are elegiac, breathing sorrow and regret, and lamenting the sacrifice of noble lives. But they are notably wanting in that fierce, revengeful tone and exultation in destruction which characterize French and German war poems. There is in the "Commemoration Ode" a solemn organ tone of exalted meditation and fervid outbursts of patriotism, but no martial strain arousing enthusiasm and glorifying the warriors' deeds by appeals to the savage passions. Longfellow, though he was a contemporary of all the heroes of the War, found no inspiration for his song in their deeds; while those who fought the battle of human rights in the pulpit and in Congress were cheered on by his voice. His *Poems on Slavery*—which, however, lack the rousing note and indignant ring of those of Whittier—may have done something towards awakening public sentiment in the North; but I doubt if they could ever have been very effective.

Whittier, man of peace though he is, sings much better of the wrath of God. With the exception of Mrs. Howe's "Battle Hymn of the Republic," I do not know a single poem in American literature that has the martial tread, the enthusiasm, the fury and fervor of war in anything like the same degree as the German war songs of Arndt and Körner. There are the bugle call, the blare of the trumpet, the abrupt, blood-stirring drum-tap, or the long, thunderous roll of the reveille in these poems, and you become temporarily a barbarian when you read them, thirsting for somebody's blood. They were valuable in their day, when the Germans were straining every nerve to throw off the French yoke; but to-day civilization has outgrown them, or ought to have outgrown them. They are as pernicious as an element of education as they are poetically beautiful.

We may concede that Dr. Johnson uttered a paradox when he said that patriotism was the last resort of scoundrels; though I am of opinion that this paradox has a wide application in the

United States to-day. The pseudo-patriotism which finds vent in savage denunciation and appeals to passions, happily extinct or in the process of extinction, and in absurd manufactured indignation regarding fancied slights or insults, are a mere flickering blaze among the expiring embers of sectional hate and martial sentiment. Ours is an industrial civilization, and emotions which are the products and supports of feudalism cannot long survive where all the normal agencies of life tend towards their suppression. Sentiments which at an earlier stage of social evolution were useful and necessary, are frequently at a later stage disorganizing and injurious. Among these are blind loyalty, implicit obedience, and subordination—all concomitants of the martial spirit. A people which possessed all these feudal virtues in an eminent degree would be poorly equipped for self-government. A strong sense of independence, a jealous insistence upon one's rights, a cool, vigilant, critical spirit—these are the qualities which make liberty possible and secure. It is the sense of loyalty and the ready submission required of the soldier in the field which, when transferred to civic life, produces bossism and the spoils system with all its attendant abuses. The civil service, with its one hundred thousand or one hundred and twenty thousand political workers, becomes an organized army, in which each one does the bidding of his chief; and the result is frequently the frustration of the will of the people, and in the course of time, perhaps, the loss of liberty.

But, it will be asked, what is the application of this to poetry and the fine arts? Well, the application is, perhaps, not obvious, but it is nevertheless near at hand. The sentiments which we regard as preeminently poetic are those which are most closely associated with the martial spirit. The verses which we learn to recite as boys and which most stir our hearts are those which deal with heroic feats of valor and self-sacrifice. The boy who "stood on the burning deck" was, when judged from a practical and unpoetic point of view, more of a fool than a hero; and yet we are taught to admire him. I admit that to me, too, he appears worthy of admiration; but that is because I, in common with the rest of my countrymen, am yet largely imbued with the martial spirit. I have a strong suspicion that to the citizen of the industrial democracy of the future Casabianca will seem unfit for survival, by reason of his defective sense of self-preservation. Browning's beautiful poem, "An Incident of the French Camp at Ratisbon," would not move us as it does if we did not share his instinctive estimate of Napoleon as a grand and exalted personage, because he had waded through carnage to a throne. The wounded youth who rides up before him, delivers his message, and falls dead, is an instance of extreme devotion to the martial chief and unquestioning acceptance of any fate which may befall one in carrying out his behests. But this virtue is possessed in a still higher degree by the most barbarous nations. Stanley relates that an African king, as a delicate compliment, presented him with the heads of a dozen of his own subjects whom he had just killed in his guest's honor; and these twelve unfortunates accepted death stolidly as a matter of course, and the incident made no sensation whatever. Thus the instincts of barbarism survive in civilization and are christened with new names, though they remain yet, at bottom, the same; and the sentiments engendered by social conditions which are anything but admirable may be put to nobler uses under new and improved conditions. Thus the heroism which was at first mere martial fury, became willingness to sacrifice self for the common good. And in this aspect it has a universal application in all stages of civilization. The man who labors unremittingly under obloquy and discouragement, for a reform which he thinks of vital importance to his fellow-men, displays a heroism which is far more difficult and therefore more laudable than that of the soldier who, amid the beating of drums and patriotic excitement, marches to his doom. The bravery which was first displayed upon the field of battle may, a couple of generations later, manifest itself as contempt for danger and unflinching perseverance in the defence of a righteous cause. And in this shape the martial virtues still remain fit subjects for the treatment of the poet, the painter, and the sculptor. It is in this transferred application that the American poets, as a rule, find inspiration in them; and they differ in this respect advantageously from the contemporary poets of Germany.

A question which I never weary of asking myself is this: How will industrialism, when consistently developed in all relations of life, affect the fine arts? Much of the lameness and tameness of contemporary poetry is, I think, due to the fact that the ideals of feudalism are losing their hold upon the public, and those of industrialism are yet but imperfectly understood. A very intelligent friend of mine insists that poetry is an obsolescent art, and that the democracy of the future will entirely dispense with it. Likewise he sees in the decorative purposes to which the arts are now being applied, an evidence that they will merely retain their places as trades of a higher degree, ministering to the material comforts of those who can afford to invest in superior skill. And even in this limited field, he thinks, they are destined to play a smaller and smaller part; for the tendency of the future will be towards equalization of material conditions, and legislative discrimination against those who now enjoy undue advantages in the struggle for existence. Let Mars and Apollo fight as much as they choose; the future, he says, is to belong to neither of them. It is to be the age of Vulcan. Let me add that this friend of mine is a philosophical student of history, and has no affiliation or sympathy with Henry George's Labor Party.

The argument with which I have endeavored to bring this prophecy to naught is this: there is nowhere any evidence of retrogression on a grand scale in human history. The evolution of the future, whatever temporary eclipses the arts may suffer in it, tends towards the development of a nobler type of man, and towards a higher average of well-being. But a man who should feel no responsive thrill at the contemplation of what is beautiful would be no improvement upon the very imperfect types which now inhabit the earth. Even if the time shall come when men will look back upon the nineteenth century as an era devoted to the cultus of a vanished beauty, a still remoter future will witness the resurrection of the arts in greater perfection. What kind of verse will then move the hearts of men, and what kind of painting and sculpture they will rejoice in, it is of course impossible to tell. It is a safe prediction, however, that as their intellects grow subtler, they will find pleasure in verse which makes a more direct and a severer appeal to the intellect than is the case with contemporary poetry. For I believe that the man of the coming centuries will be a more intellectual and a less emotional creature than his ancestor of to-day. Browning, in spite of the ruggedness and unmelodiousness of his verse, has, in my opinion, a long lease upon the future. The subtle psychological problems with which he deals—the marvellous soul-histories he unravels—will delight men more and more, and open paths in which others will follow. Goethe's grand and free spirit, with its many-sided development, points in other directions to new problems, new struggles, and peaceful victories. These two names are to me the guide-posts into the dim land of the poetry of the future.

1888

PHILISTINISM

TO Matthew Arnold belongs the credit of having anglicized and popularized the German word *Philister*.* England, the home *par excellence* of Philistinism, did not need the term before the apostle of sweetness and light had preached his gospel, because the vanishing fraction of the British nation which was not Philistine did not feel themselves, as yet, as a superior intellectual caste, and, therefore, lacked the temerity to differentiate themselves from the worshippers of Mammon. Perhaps they even aspired to be classed among those whom they despised, or, if they

---

* My friend Col. T. W. Higginson informs me that the word "Philistine" was employed in the German sense by Margaret Fuller d'Ossoli and other writers for the *Dial*, the organ of American transcendentalism.

did not, their wives did; for the children of light have from days of old had a fatal propensity for marrying the daughters of the Philistines, who are no less captivating now than they were in the times of Joshua and Gideon. And they have the same trick yet of underestimating the blessings of their new condition, and longing back on the sly for the tribe of their fathers, in the land of Philistia.

A Philistine, in the German sense — it may not be superfluous to state — is a dweller in Grub Street, a person who has no interests beyond his material welfare, whose mental horizon is circumscribed, the wings of whose fancy rarely rise above bread and butter. No divine discontent, no aspiration, no torturing doubts trouble the Philistine bosom. As long as his ledgers balance and his digestion is unimpaired he is satisfied with the universe, satisfied with himself, and pities the fool who worries about problems in a world that is provided with so many good things to eat and drink. A university education, by furnishing a man with intellectual interests, is supposed to lift him out of his native Philistinism; and German student songs are full of exultation in this fact, and of contempt for the sordid materialism of the Philistines. That there are academical Philistines quite as sordid, unaspiring, and stolidly contented as their *confrères* in trade and commerce, is, perhaps, beginning to be recognized; but as it is not an inspiring theme for poetry, the song-book may be pardoned for classing all academical citizens among the children of light. The aristocracy of culture is, in the land of the Teutons, a very much greater power than we, on this side of the Atlantic, imagine; and the Philistine, accordingly, is a trifle more modest and makes less noise.

If we would see the Philistine full-blown in the flower of his perfection, we must cross to the British Isles. There he rules not only the wave but the dry land as well; and makes life as uncomfortable as possible for every one who is disposed to find fault with him. With all due regard for the many grand spirits which Great Britain has produced, I doubt if any truer verdict could be passed upon the nation, as a whole, than that of Matthew Arnold: "An upper class materialized, a middle class vulgarized, a lower class brutalized." That means, in other words, that (with some illustrious exceptions, who serve but to prove the rule) the whole nation is Philistine, though in varying degrees.

Let any one who wishes to convince himself of this fact read the lives of the English poets. How terribly, how cruelly non-conformism, in every instance, has been punished, and how promptly conformism (even if coupled with mediocre attainments) has been rewarded. John Bull holds himself the tuning-fork, and forces his poets to sing in the key which he chooses to demand. They may enjoy considerable latitude in that key; but let them beware, if they stray into one of their own choosing. The fates of Shelley and Byron (the former, with all his aberrations, a most noble spirit) are a perpetual warning to British bards who might be inclined to "follow too much the devices and desires of their own hearts;" and those of Wordsworth and Southey advertise a premium to him who abandons the hope of the promised land and returns to the flesh-pots of Egypt. It is to be conceded, perhaps, that the British Philistine is, in this respect, a trifle less exacting than formerly; granting men like Swinburne, for instance, without any extreme penalty, the liberty to rave melodiously about a revolutionary sunrise which he professes to espy upon the misty horizon. But then Swinburne is a poet for the few, and can never be sufficiently popular to be dangerous. Even his complicated canzonettes and ballades and villanelles about babies' shoes and stockings appeal chiefly to those who are unacquainted with these articles in the original. Let him only venture, if he could, to sing revolution to tunes as popular as those of Tom Moore's "Irish Melodies," and we should see what would happen.

I believe Great Britain is the only land of an advanced civilization where the Philistine spirit is so dominant, even in the universities, as to be able to exclude the greatest scholars from the academic chairs on account of their religious non-conformism. In Germany the universities are engaged in a sharp competition for the possession of scientists like Helmholtz, Virchow, and Dubois-Reymond; and it occurs to no one to inquire what may be their opinions on theology. In France, likewise, it has been the custom to attach scientific pioneers like Claude Bernard, Pasteur, and Charcot to the Sorbonne or the Collège de France, the latter institution being founded expressly for the encouragement of independent research without reference to accepted tradition. It would be difficult, I fancy, in France as in Germany to find any really great name in science which was not connected with some seat of learning. But in England the two great universities, Oxford and Cambridge, have cheerfully dispensed with the services of men like Darwin, Herbert Spencer, Tyndall, Huxley, Faraday, Sir Humphry Davy, nay, of wellnigh all the illustrious banner-bearers of modern progress; and gloried, in the meanwhile, in their Puseys and Newmans and Mannings—all most excellent men, but, at heart, mediævalists and utterly out of sympathy with the nineteenth century, for which (whatever be its failings) it is the business of universities to educate its students. I am not by any means sure that Darwin or any of his *confrères* would have accepted a call from Oxford or Cambridge; but if they had all refused, it would have been because of this theological mediævalism to which I have referred. Scientific research never flourishes in such an atmosphere. I am not sure that the late Mark Pattison, M. P., in his report to the British Parliament, ascribed the comparative failure of Oxford and Cambridge to educate live modern men in a modern spirit to the clerical Toryism which then pervaded the air of those venerable institutions;* but I remember vividly his declaration that the smallest German university, with its underpaid professors and half-starved *privat docenten*, accomplishes more for learning

---

* I am aware that Oxford and Cambridge have greatly changed since the above was written. *Vide* Goldwin Smith's article "Oxford Revisited," in the *Fortnightly* for February, 1894. "Oxford," says this author, "is now exceedingly sensitive to the charge of not being abreast of the age."

than Oxford and Cambridge with their magnificent endowments.*

Some years ago I had the pleasure of making the acquaintance of the French Philistine; and since I am dealing with his tribe, I cannot, for reasons of politeness, omit mentioning what an interesting acquaintance I found him to be. The French Philistine is named collectively Joseph Prudhomme, and is, on the whole, not a bad fellow. He has none of the brutality towards his inferiors of his neighbor beyond the Channel; nor his snobbish servility towards his superiors. He is a small *bourgeois*, absorbed in petty economies, and the chief aim of his life is to make both ends meet. He is a terrific Chauvinist, and believes that nothing admirable can originate outside of France. But the Southern sun has brightened his temper and made it kindly and genial. He takes his pleasure like a civilized being, and not like a morose and besotted brute. If his intellect is not very alert, a certain emotional vivacity serves

* Quoted from memory.

him as a fair substitute for intellect. He
feels himself intensely as a member of *la
grande nation;* and the heritage of the
Revolution (even though he may not at
all comprehend it) has stimulated his self-
esteem and given him a certain human
dignity which his *confrères* in other lands
usually lack. I am speaking of the class
of French Philistines, as a whole, includ-
ing the small traders and shopkeepers in
Paris and the provincial cities, who live
decent lives, make their families fairly
happy, and hold the government responsible for the crops and the state of trade.
A thousand years ago it was the fashion
to cut the king's head off when the crops
were poor; and in France, as we all know,
the fashion has been illustrated in recent
times. The Philistine, in all lands, judges
his government to this day by the crops
it makes and the state of trade; and
that is one of the advantages which a
republic has over a monarchy, that you
cannot, except metaphorically, cut its
head off when it fails to regulate the
weather satisfactorily. Like the hydra, it
grows new heads as fast as you cut the

old ones off; and each new growth is apt to be uglier than the preceding one.

Now, as regards the American Philistine, I have been told by professed connoisseurs that he does not exist. Ah, would that it were so! But I run my head against him most unexpectedly every day; and as his head is harder than mine, I am the sufferer by the collision. At the time when he flew into a rage over Mrs. Trollope's libel, and grew hysterical over the caricatures by Charles Dickens (my friends say), then the American Philistine was a dominant type; but now he is as extinct as the megatherium, except in Chicago, where he yet survives and grows rich on pork. But, friends, let us bear in mind our definition. A Philistine is a worshipper of Mammon—a person destitute of higher interests. Look about among your acquaintances, and you will be astonished at the number you will find whom the cap fits. I have the misfortune to meet quite frequently an opulent member of the tribe who pats me patronizingly on the shoulder, asks me how much I make by my writings, tells me, by way of contrast, how much he made last week by a single transaction in wheat; and while I laugh at him in my sleeve, he basks, as he imagines, in my envious admiration. His chief pride is that he has made his own living since he was twelve years old; when he commenced his illustrious career by sweeping out his father's store. If he takes me to drive, he tells me how much his horses cost. He is so sublimely unconscious of his bad taste that it would be sheer waste of energy to grow angry with him, and I conclude by despising myself for suffering such patronage without resentment. As for intellectual interests, he does not know what the term means, and he does not care to know. All that which lies beyond his mental horizon is embraced in his stolid and capacious contempt.

I am sure you know this type as well as I do. Perhaps you have also made a discovery upon which I have prided myself, viz., that the American Philistine does not invariably propagate his kind. His son, it is an even chance, will desert the tribe, and attach himself to the tribe which his father despises. This is a case of rapid intellectual evolution which seems to be confined to our continent. The English and the German Philistine remain Philistine generation after generation, differing only in the degree and odiousness of their Philistinism. Joseph Prudhomme, too, is blessed with a multitude of small Prudhommes, who, in their turn, are apt to be similarly blessed. But the American worshipper of Baal has apparently at the bottom of his inner consciousness a sneaking suspicion that he is, perhaps, after all, not so admirable as he has fondly imagined; that there may, after all, be something worth considering in the things which he affects to despise; and, accordingly, he will give his son the chance to determine for himself what the value of these things may be. A college career of four years may or may not enlighten the young man on this subject; he may relapse into his native Philistinism like the German *Brodstudenten*, to whom science is nothing but a means of earning his livelihood. But the chances are against such a relapse; in an experience of fourteen years I have known but few instances. The tribe of the Philistines in the United States are not deficient in cerebral development, and if a higher outlook is once opened in their minds, it is not probable that it will ever be closed.

What is true of the sons of the Philistines is no less true of their daughters; although the educational opportunities that are provided for the latter are usually so poor that no stimulus to higher interests is derived from school or college. But the daughters of the Philistines are blessed with an abundance of leisure; they are, in fact, the only leisured class of the United States; and for want of better things to do, they fill the yawning vacuums of their days with novel-reading. The greater part of what they read is shockingly bad; but occasionally they stumble upon a good book, which makes a miniature revolution in their miniature brains. How often I have witnessed this sudden awakening of a young woman's mind, which had slumbered contentedly or discontentedly for a period of years. Then comes a hunger for culture which is truly pathetic—an omnivorous consumption of novels, histories, critical essays, and scientific speculation. The eagerness with which these damsels seek intellectual guidance, and follow every erratic will-o'-the-wisp that dances away over swamps and quagmires, is another pathetic phenomenon, which is constantly repeating itself within the sphere of my observation. The Philistine home which concerns itself only with food, drink, clothes, and social prestige, fails to supply to the children that mental balance which is only to be found in true culture gradually imparted from early years, and religious principles vitally pervading the domestic life.

No portrait of the American Philistine would be complete without some reference to his behavior abroad. It is a piece of national good-fortune, or misfortune, according as you choose to view it, that our Philistine is rich. He can afford to travel, and when travelling he likes to make himself as conspicuous as possible. He brags of his opulence, patronizes the effete monarchies, whose manners (which he designates as "frills"), customs, and institutions fill him with a grand patriotic contempt. He discourses loudly in the reading-rooms of the banks and exchanges on the superiority of the United States and all that appertains to them to Europe and all that appertains to it, and makes himself generally obnoxious. To Europe he represents America; is the typical American, and cheerfully accepts his representative character. It is futile for us who refuse to recognize him in this capacity to protest that he libels his native land. The only way to make him harmless would be to keep him at home; and as this is impossible, we have no choice but to submit with good grace to his misrepresentation.

1888

SOME STRAY NOTES ON ALPHONSE DAUDET

THERE is no novelist living who possesses the quality of charm in a higher degree than Alphonse Daudet. His phrases have a degree of felicity which make him the despair of translators. Compared to him even such accomplished writers as Clarétie and Guy de Maupassant seem a trifle heavy-handed. It is difficult to see how the mere art of expression can be carried to a greater height than he has carried it. His pages abound in winged words, which the reader (if he be sufficiently skilled in the vernacular to perceive their exquisite flavor) sits and gloats over and returns to with fresh delight. But these winged words — butterfly-winged words, one might almost call them—are so light and delicate that they are apt to lose their color and perfume in the hands of the translator. Who, for instance, could ever hope (though, we believe, more than one has had the boldness to try) to transfer into another tongue that maze of sun-steeped Southern phrases, redolent of "dance and Provençal song and sunburnt mirth" which are collected under the title *Lettres de mon Moulin?* *L'Arlesienne*, for instance, or *La Belle Nivernaise*—who would have the hardihood to say that he could put that into adequate English?

The question as to whether Daudet is a realist or a romanticist has been debated in France without any decisive result as far as the public is concerned. A realist in the sense that Zola is, or claims to be, a realist he surely is not, though there is evidence in his latest novels—notably *Sapho* and *L'Evangéliste*—that Zola's laurels disturb his sleep. Whatever value his books have, apart from their mere charm of style, surely rests upon their fidelity to actual conditions. Daudet set out deliberately to be the literary historiographer of the Second Empire, just as Balzac had been that of the kingdom of Louis Philippe, *le roi citoyen*. His position as private secretary to the Duc de Morny afforded him an excellent opportunity for studying that age of glittering corruption in its most intimate aspects. Never was an embryonic novelist more happily placed than Alphonse Daudet in the bed-chamber (for the duke conducted most of his affairs from his bed-chamber) of that dazzling, fascinating, unscrupulous, amiable, and altogether complex libertine who ruled France in the name of his half-brother, Napoleon III. But, on the other hand, it is doubtful if France at that time possessed another man so happily equipped for making the most of this rare opportunity. Read *The Nabob* and you will be able to judge. There is the social record of the Second Empire, written in letters of flame. Though concessions are made to the exigencies of art, the book is almost a chronicle, and a *chronique scandaleuse* at that, as every novel of the period was bound to be. It gathers the striking characteristics of that interesting *décadence* into a large, impressive, and comprehensive picture. Natural causes produce natural — nay, inevitable — effects. We get a view of the hidden levers and springs which set all this complex machinery in motion; and, though it may not increase our respect for the Empire to know what these springs were, it certainly will increase our knowledge and understanding of many bewildering facts of modern history. All the mushroom growths which flourished and luxuriated in those days on the dunghill of official corruption, and whose soil was blown from under them by the explosion of the Franco-Prussian war, fill, perhaps, a disproportionate space in the story; and, in order to spare the sensibilities of the sentimental reader at the final catastrophe, the author has introduced one pure and innocent pair of lovers—M. de Gerry and Mademoiselle Joyeuse—who, like a modern Deucalion and Pyrrha, are saved in a water-tight little compartment amid the universal deluge.

Of Daudet's other novels, *Le Petit*

Chose, which was the first in order, is particularly attractive by reason of the biographical material which it contains. Up to the eleventh chapter it is a truthful account of the author's boyhood and early youth. Its tone is sentimental and a trifle lachrymose. Daudet is the son of a once-prosperous silk manufacturer in Nismes, who failed, moved to Lyons, where the son's troubles began, and never recovered his peace of mind or his fortune. His father's poverty and ill-humor were sore trials to Alphonse; and his sensitive temperament and lack of pluck (in the Anglo-Saxon sense) caused him to feel the misfortunes of his family with an acuteness which made his boyhood, after the removal from the sunny South, a perpetual misery. Read the vivid chapter in *Le Petit Chose* on the hunt for the cockroaches in the dreary lodgings in Lyons. It bears the indelible stamp of autobiography, and is altogether masterly in its grim veracity. If it had been venomous serpents the Eysette family had been hunting for in corners and crevices, the author could not have expended more horror on the situation. The temperamental note which is here so distinctly struck vibrates audibly through all the early books of the author. In *Jack*, which is a prolonged misery in some thirty-odd chapters, the hero becomes positively tiresome by reason of his misfortunes. If his various miseries were not described with such marvellous vividness that it becomes an artistic pleasure to follow them, we should cheerfully renounce the acquaintance of Master Jack and his reprehensible mother at an early stage of their career. But Jack's mother is the kind of character which it is not easy to dismiss. Flippant, vicious, goodnatured, sentimental, and by turns affectionate and cruel, she is so altogether modern and contemporaneous in all her contradictory characteristics that her follies become interesting by reason of being typical. There is a strong flavor of Dickens in this novel, as also in the description of the Joyeuse family in *The Nabob;* and it would seem probable that the author of *David Copperfield* and *Dombey and Son* had inspired a good many chapters in Daudet, if the latter did not expressly declare that he has never read Dickens, or at least had not read him at the time when these novels were written.

If Daudet had remained faithful to a resolution which at a certain time of his life he no doubt cherished, we should have missed the works by which he will be longest remembered; viz., *Fromont jeune et Risler aîné* (English, *Sidonie*) and *Numa Roumestan*. For if he had confined himself to depicting the Second Empire in all its phases—its *comédie humaine*, in the Balzac sense—he would have been compelled to leave the Republic to the tender mercies of some more or less competent successor. It is generally assumed (though Daudet has taken pains to deny it) that Numa Roumestan is none other than Gambetta, and that in the face of a hundred denials he will continue to remain Gambetta. It is easy to understand how a novelist can with safe conscience depict a man, and yet say that the result is not a portrait. An artist like Daudet refrains from servile copying, but he takes the kernel of a man's character, his essential nature, as it were, and clothes it in living flesh and blood; adhering, no doubt, to the actual type which he has in mind, but adding touches here and there and inventing traits and incidents which are in essential harmony with the character. The result, then, both is and is not the same as the living model. Daudet has in this sense denied that the Duc de Mora in *The Nabob* is intended to represent the Duc de Morny, and he might with equal propriety deny that he is himself The Little Thing in *Le Petit Chose*. As a matter of fact, there is probably not a single prominent character (nay, perhaps not even a subordinate one) in all Daudet's books which is not drawn from a living model. He has very little invention of the romantic sort (in which, for instance, Dumas *père* excelled). He is, in my opinion, a better novelist for not having it. His books are historic documents of unimpeachable value. To the future historian of the Second Empire and the Third Republic they will be of greater importance than any number of diplomatic blue-books and protocols of legislative proceedings. Thus people thought and acted in France in the latter half of the nineteenth century; every page bears evidence of the author's veracity. These are the typical characters in politics, religion, society, finance, and trade. The lower strata of society he has neglected, obviously because he does not know them. It is only Parisian life which he knows and by preference describes. If he is ever to rival Balzac in comprehensiveness and completeness (as he surpasses him in delicacy and felicity of phrase), he will have to write novels dealing with the *Vie de Province* before he is many years older, though he may without offence omit the *Études Philosophiques*. But it is an open question whether Balzac added to his laurels by his novels of provincial life, and we fear Daudet would, outside of his native South, suffer a worse fate. His *Tartarin de Tarascon* is a revelation of the very heart of the florid, magniloquent South of France; the sunny, luxuriant South, with its love of glory, its half-burlesque yearning for heroism, its sweet *naïveté*, and its indestructible joy in existence. To have depicted this ought to suffice for any man's ambition.

Of Daudet's other works *The Kings in Exile* is the most notable. The King of Illyria, who, having lost his crown by a revolution, wastes his health and substance in riotous living, while his heroic wife plots and schemes for the recovery of his throne, is but a thin disguise for the King of Naples, whose fate and personality in nowise differed from those of the unworthy scion of royalty who is here described. *The Evangelist* is a somewhat repulsive study of religious fanaticism, and gives one the impression that the author is here in an unknown territory, where he has not. as yet, taken his bearings. In *Sapho* we find Daudet entering into rivalry with Zola in his own field. How a man of fifty who is a father can dedicate such a book to his sons "when they will be twenty years old" is a mystery which it takes a Frenchman to understand.

Henry James, if I remember rightly,

once sighed for more latitude in English fiction, but I fancy that if he had been a Frenchman (and still been Henry James) he would have sighed for less. It would seem impossible to go farther than Daudet has done in *Sapho* and still remain within the domain of literature. Zola's *Nana* is, morally speaking, a saner and healthier book. No one will ever rise from its perusal without the same sort of shudder which he might feel at witnessing a clinic or an autopsy. And Zola, by the way, in describing his heroine as a pest-boil on the body social, frankly assumes the rôle of a demonstrator. He is, indeed, no mean pathologist, whatever one may think of his psychology. Daudet, on the other hand, is primarily an artist, and as such necessarily a psychologist. From his dedication it is to be surmised that he meant incidentally, or at least inferentially, to preach. But his sermon resembles those of Abraham à Santa Clara. It is so clever, so witty, so amusing, that one is apt to overlook its moral import. While *Nana* warns and frightens, *Sapho* piques one's curiosity. The charm of the very improper heroine is so delicately insinuated that the reader has to be on his guard against a sneaking desire for her acquaintance. He does not loathe her as he does Nana. He is not shaken in his innermost being at the contemplation of her destructiveness to body and soul. The beautiful Gorgon whom Zola has depicted is therefore far less dangerous than the beautiful Siren of his subtile and exquisite *confrère*.

Of *The Immortal* I shall not say much, because I have not read it. Although a professional reviewer, I have not yet acquired that oracular infallibility which enables so many members of my guild to say striking things about books which they have not read. A friend of mine who habitually bristles with epigram, informs me that it is a most profound exposition of the shallowness of modern life, a most noble disquisition upon its meanness, and a most civilized demonstration of our imminent return to savagery. In other words, it is a discourse upon the fierceness of the modern struggle for existence; and its hero is aptly designated by that awful specimen of a Gallicised anglicism, *le struggle for lifeur*. The plot hinges upon a hotly-contested election to the "Society of the Forty Immortals," the French Academy.

The History of My Books, which is delightfully confidential, is full of the "sweetness and light" of the author's early period. It discreetly lifts the veil of privacy, and gives us pleasant glimpses of his personality and family relations. It is of light weight compared to *The Nabob* and *Numa Roumestan;* but, apart from the excellence of its literary workmanship, it is interesting as showing that, like those of Goethe, Daudet's works are but "one continued confession." "Blood is a quite peculiar juice," says Mephistopheles; and every book of lasting value is written with its author's blood. Such books can never grow old, and, even when the age has outgrown them, they will preserve a vitality which will save them from oblivion.

Artists' Wives is a collection of short stories which no artist candidate for matrimony can afford to leave unread. It is an elaboration in twelve chapters of Punch's laconic advice: "Don't." The preface, which is an ingenious bit of dialogue between a poet and a painter, the former a bachelor and the latter happily married, would, in spite of its cautious reservations and concessions, deprive even a Brigham Young of his taste for marrying. To steer safely in such dangerous waters, where hidden rocks and quicksands lie in wait to wreck your frail bark at every turn of your rudder, would require a firmer hand, a cooler head, and a deeper knowledge of navigation than even the most conceited male would pretend to possess. When the vulgarly clever and pretty shop-girl ruins the life of the promising poet, Heurtesbise, it might seem to the uninitiated that Heurtesbise got no more than his deserts, if he was fool enough to take a pretty face on trust—and out of a bric-à-brac shop at that. But, unhappily, that is the kind of folly for which not only young poets but young men in all professions have a fatal proclivity. It is indeed well that men should marry in their foolish age, or they would not marry at all — in the upper strata of society, I mean, where women have, as a rule, ceased to be helpmeets to their husbands, as they yet generally are in the lower ranks.

But Daudet (leaving the question in its wider bearings out of consideration) desires merely to enforce the proposition that an artist runs a far greater risk than do other men in marrying. He absolutely requires for his happiness that his wife shall love his art, and be interested in the æsthetic, and not merely the commercial aspects of his occupation. But women who are by training and temperament capable of this æsthetic appreciation would seem to be very rare in France, if we are to judge by Daudet's book. The *petites misères* of daily companionship with an unbeloved or uncongenial partner he depicts with a convincing mastery and vividness which lifts them, as it were, into the region of actual experience, and he accomplishes this result by those felicitous feather-touches of description and portraiture which are so peculiarly his own that they would seem to require a new adjective for their characterization, coined from his name.

Altogether, the score of novels which bear the name of Alphonse Daudet will prove most precious documents to the future historian who shall undertake to do for the nineteenth century what Taine, Thiers, and De Tocqueville have done for the eighteenth.

MY LOST SELF

IF Mr. Thomas Hardy had not appropriated the title *The Return of the Native*, I should have employed it as a superscription for the following reflections. There is a suggestion in the word "native" which I particularly like—a flavor of the woods—of something indigenous, aboriginal, deeply rooted in the soil. It was the feeling that I had in a measure forfeited the right to apply it to myself which caused me a vague heartache during my recent visit to Norway. A residence of twenty-three years in the United States had so completely transformed me — changed my very substance — that I lacked the brazenness even to personate my lost Norse self. I knew beforehand that it would have been a dismal failure. It is not your physical fibres only that are perpetually displaced and renewed; your spiritual being is subject to the same cruel and beneficent law of renovation and decay; and it is a very singular sensation to be suddenly made aware (as I was in Norway) of what you had changed from—to be confronted, as it were, with your lost, primitive self. I met him (should I say *it?*) on the pier the moment I set foot on Norwegian soil. He shook me by the hand, stared at me with a sharp reproach, and remarked that I "affected a foreign accent." He spoke Norwegian to my wife and sons, and was filled with amazement, not unmixed with reprobation, because they did not understand him.

"What!" he asked, in a tone of rebuke; "do you mean to say that you have not taught your children your mother tongue?"

I explained apologetically that it was not their mother tongue, and that they had had no opportunity of learning it; whereupon I sank so low in the estimation of my lost self that we barely managed with great stress to be polite to each other.

The doubt tormented me, during the first week of my sojourn in Norway, whether my lost self might not, after all, be right. I went into book-stores, dry-goods stores, and telegraph-offices, delivering myself, as I fancied, of the most elegant Norwegian, and everywhere the man in charge either answered me in English, or called a clerk who possessed the accomplishment of English speech. I cudgelled my brain to find out what was the matter with my Norwegian, and received at last a succinct explanation from a friend, who asserted that there was nothing at all the matter with it except that it was English. It was, he said, the kind of Norwegian that is spoken by Englishmen and Americans — only, perhaps, a trifle more fluent. How curiously this intimation affected me no one will comprehend. A sort of somnambulistic confusion of identity haunted me. I saw things from two distinct points of view. I saw myself dimly, as I appeared to my lost self, and viewed myself with sentiments of mingled contempt and pity, and at the same time I reciprocated his feelings cordially; and from the mental elevation of a man of the world, who had taken a cosmopolitan survey of humanity, I looked down upon him as a simple-minded, patriotic little cockney. Now I was my lost self, and shared his sentiments; and now, again, I was my new American self, who regarded things Norwegian with something of the interested superciliousness with which a big and rich nation patronizes a small and poor one. If this perpetual flitting between my two selves, with its attendant conflicts of sentiment, had continued long enough, I should, no doubt, by a psychological necessity have been torn into two distinct beings — a Norwegian Jekyl and an American Hyde, or an American Jekyl and a Norwegian Hyde; and we should have ended by parting as amicably as circumstances would permit, though I fancy a mysterious interdependence of each upon the other—a haunting sense of incompleteness, and perhaps a mutual homesick yearning—would scarcely be avoided.

A reminiscence from my childhood, which had been banished from my mind for a quarter of a century, returned to me with extreme vividness and caused me the liveliest regret. When I was nine or ten years old I had a tutor, of the ultra-patriotic species known as Norse-Norseman. Once when we were standing together on the beach, looking at the huge mountain peaks reflected in the fiord, he broke forth with startling suddenness.

"Boy," he said, with a noble glow of enthusiasm, "the first thing you should thank God for in the morning and the last thing at night is this, that you are born a Norwegian. God made no end of Frenchmen and Germans and Englishmen, but he made only a very few Norwegians, *because the stuff was too precious.*"

Never shall I forget the thrill of patriotic pride which rippled through me at the consciousness that I belonged to this select and favored race. How with a boy's delight in the heroic I gloried in the feats of the Vikings on sea and land, the bloodier the better; and with a savage joy in adventure depicted to myself their brave galleys sailing the main, and spreading terror of the Norseman's name throughout the effete kingdoms of the world. How heartlessly I joined in deriding and tormenting those boys at school whose appellations indicated an admixture of Dutch, Danish, or German blood! How deeply I despised them; how mercilessly I made them feel their inferiority to the proud Norseman! I remember with what righteous indignation I once thrashed a boy as a mere wholesome discipline because his father was a Dane; for the Danes, as I had recently learned from history, were the enemies of Norway, and had maltreated her for four hundred years, once even reducing her to a provincial relation. I had an old score to settle on my country's behalf, and I settled it then and there. Never have I felt so virtuous, so gloriously contented as I did when, with my hands in my pocket, I swaggered away from that weeping Danish boy. I felt I was playing an historic rôle and was justifying my noble ancestry. It is nearly thirty years since I performed this heroic feat, and I blush to think how miserably I have since degenerated! Now, like the cosmopolitan poltroon I am, I bow politely to mine enemies and make flattering speeches to those who despitefully use me. It never occurs to me to avenge my country's wrongs by boxing the ears of any chance gentleman whose ancestors may have been mixed up with the ancient feuds of Norway. But for all that, I feel a sort of amused tenderness for this lost juvenile self of mine, and I would give a year of my life to be able to transpose myself back into that noble piratical state of mind, when to swing a cutlass seemed so infinitely more glorious than to be driving a quill.

I shall, in all likelihood, be suspected of levity if I say that I would contentedly return to that primitive condition, and count myself thrice blessed if, by some magic process, I could slip back permanently into my lost self; if I could drink deeply of that potion of oblivion which Grimhild in the Volsunga Saga gave to

Sigurd, and have all the experience that has transformed me drift away and vanish like a dream that dissolves at waking. The world was not draped in gray then, but lay dewy and fragrant, flushed with the lovely colors of the dawn. What a passion of life and joy thrilled in my veins! How melodiously my heart beat! And how brave, how strenuous, how ravishing its rhythm! How remote from me was the dreary resignation, the melancholy philosophy of patience which now weighs like a gray deposit of the current of time upon my spirit! Nay, there was a zest in each breath—a wholesome savage relish in the taste and feel and smell of things, for the loss of which no bookish delights can compensate. And what an exquisite set of senses I had, forsooth! How keen-edged, quiveringly alert, and vigilant they were! I could almost weep (if that too were not one of my lost accomplishments) at the thought of all the happiness that I have forfeited by the gradual blunting of those delicate instruments for apprehending reality. How sweet the world smelled every morning, when it woke with a bright, dewy gaze from the slumber of the night! How I plunged into it, revelled, rioted in it with wanton zest! Each season had its own peculiar joys. There was an inexhaustible delight in watching the changing tone of earth and sky at the approach of spring; and scarcely less was the rapture with which I hailed the autumnal splendors—the first frost on the river and the birds of passage and the first premonitions of snow.

I maintain that no pleasure that life has offered me in later years is comparable to these; and it was because my lost self was temporarily revived and persisted in nudging me in the side wherever I went; it was therefore, I say, that my anticipated enjoyments assumed such an elegiac tone — nay, were largely turned into regrets. I was like an organist who sits down at his instrument to play Mendelssohn's Wedding March, and whose fingers wander away, willy-nilly, into the solemn intricacies of the Dead March in "Saul." I sat down, in my American self, at an American desk, filled with patronizing superciliousness towards my Norse self; and lo and behold! my Norse self slipped into the seat of consciousness, and, like Balaam, I find that my curses have turned into blessings. I fancied, until this fatal visit to Norway, that I was greatly to be congratulated on having risen in the scale of civilization; but now I would willingly descend the scale again, step by step, or at one grand stride, if I could be sure of recovering what I have lost.

My American self, who has been silenced in this debate, here mildly insinuates that I have been guilty of a confusion of terms. It is not, in the opinion of this authority, my primitive self, but my youth I am regretting. All these delightful things which unquestionably have gone from me I should have lost as surely, with the lapse of years, if I had remained primitive. I am in the position of the poet in the prologue to "Faust," and my yearnings, as well as their cause, are identical with his:

"Then give me back that time of pleasures,
    When yet in joyous growth I sang;

When, like a fount, the thronging measures
  Uninterrupted gushed and sprang!
Then bright mist veiled the world before
    me;
  In opening buds a marvel woke,
  As I the thousand blossoms broke,
Which every valley richly bore me!
  I nothing had, and yet enough for
    youth—
  Joy in illusion, ardent thirst for truth.
Give, unrestrained, the old emotion,
  The bliss that touched the verge of pain,
The strength of Hate, Love's deep devo-
    tion—
  O give me back my youth again!"

If I were capable of detaching myself from my American self as completely as I did a year ago, I should make a crushing rejoinder to this insinuation; but suffering, as I do, from the old confusion of identity, I shall have to leave it unanswered.

1892

THE MERIDIAN OF LIFE

TO pass the meridian of life — the half-way house, the temporary resting-place between youth and age—is an unpleasant thing. I never yet knew a man who did it joyously. An elegiac mood seems the proper one for the occasion. A melancholy resignation invades one's spirit on that fatal day, in spite of one's resolve to take a cheerful view of the situation. Though you may laugh ever so heartily, and be as youthfully frisky as you like, there is apt to be a slightly forced note in your mirth, and your jaunty demeanor is a trifle conscious and lacks the charm of heedless spontaneity which made you so irresistible to the ladies in your younger days. You may put a bold face upon it, and brazenly assert that you feel as young as ever.

Nobody will believe you, dear friend. I do not believe you, and, what is worse, you do not believe yourself. If youth only meant a cheerful acceptance of life as it is, a readiness to join in gayety and innocent pleasures, a capacity for falling in love, etc., then I don't in the least doubt that you are young, though you may be past the meridian. But these are merely the superficial characteristics of youth. The deeper ones are as subtle as perfumes and as hard to catch. When they depart, they depart finally and forever. They are beyond simulation and imitation. And the fact is that no middle-aged man, wishing to appear young, would ever dream of simulating them.

The first (though the order is arbitrary) is a certain emotional exuberance, a certain rank ferment of the blood, which prompts vehement sentiment and headlong, inconsiderate action. It is what Swinburne celebrates under the terms "foam" and "froth" and "mist," and it is what imparted an indefinable charm to his early verses. It was the warm and riotous pulse of youth; and since, without any complicity on his part, this has departed from him, he is not half the poet he was before. Middle age has shorn him of the locks of his strength. It is the rhythmic vehemence or the vehement rhythm of our blood which, at that happy period, makes poets of most of us. It is at that time that prose is too slow and pale and commonplace to express our emotions, and with the sweet unconsciousness of young birds we set about imitating the older singers. Oh, the divine folly of those years! How I luxuriated in fictitious love and remorse and despair! How absorbingly interesting I found myself, while I was harboring all these emotions and relieving my overburdened heart in poems which, when I read them now, seem positively humorous. How unblushingly I borrowed from Goethe, from Tennyson, but above all from Heine, who is the poet *par excellence* of unhappy love. The young lady with whom, for want of a better subject, I enacted this serio-comic tragedy, was a prosaic soul, and I strongly suspect that I really cared very little about her; but I needed some one to be unhappily in love with, and she seemed to be the only available candidate for the position. There was in my breast a large store of accumulated sentiment which I had to expend upon somebody.

Turguéneff once said to me, in response to an inquiry about his health: "Oh, I am getting old, and I know it by one infallible test. I try to be cheerful. I cherish my pleasant emotions. When I was young it was my gloomy sentiments I revelled in. It was my despair which nourished my self-respect. It was melancholy, remorse for imagined sins, hopeless love, which I cherished with particular satisfaction."

This remark did not at all strike me as profound at the time I heard it. I was then on the sunny side of the meridian, and incapable of philosophizing concerning my own condition. "What a pity," I thought, "that so great a man should be so cynical."

And forthwith I spun a lurid romance about him out of such material as I had at my command, and concluded that his cynicism was the result of a disappointed or unrequited love. (I have learned since that it was the result of a lavishly requited love.) But now that I have passed the meridian, I find myself verifying his experience. I surprise myself pushing (with a prosaic impatience) unpleasant subjects out of sight; subjects which ten or twenty years ago would have given me material for the most delightfully gloomy meditations and sage entries in my diary concerning the bitterness of love, the insignificance of life, the futility of all human endeavor. Such scant emotions as I now have I allow to pass without apostrophizing them or photographing them in a diary, or in any wise detailing them; and if, by chance, I stumble upon one which it seems worth while to prolong, it is sure to be a cheerful one. My stories, which, in a sense, I wrote with my heart-blood (and no story is worth anything which is written with a cheaper liquid), had, by some strange, occult necessity, to end unhappily. Most of my heroes, in those days, had tragic experiences. I marvel, in retrospect, that a humane, kind-hearted man (as I believe I am) could have heaped up so much gratuitous misery. One handsome and deserving young man, who never had harmed a fly, I induced to sit down and freeze to death on the front stoop under the window of his beloved. Another I condemned to a kind of roving vagabondage, like the Wandering Jew, all owing to a sentimental affliction; and a third wore out his life miserably in an effort to restore sight to the girl whom he loved. A fiendish ingenuity assisted me in inventing distressing situations, from which there seemed no issue possible except death by frost or fire or a long self-imposed martyrdom of sorrow and suffering. Problems which to heroic and uncompromising youth seem insoluble, differences which seem irreconcilable, may to middle age, with its easy, *laissez-faire* philosophy, seem not at all hopeless. The stoic of twenty frequently becomes an epicurean at forty. Young Goethe could see no possible fate but death for Werther, enamoured of his friend's *fiancée;* but the middle-aged publisher, Nicolai, subjected the sentimental hero to medical treatment, and by liberal cupping dispelled his romantic fantasies, until his reason reasserted itself. And in the end he made a rich and sensible match, and became the father of a large and blooming family.

In no book with which I am acquainted is the subtle process, incident upon the passing of the meridian of life, more truthfully and delightfully depicted than in *An Indian Summer*, by W. D. Howells. It is not the occasional twinge of rheumatism, or the weariness after the ball, or an inclination to drowsiness after dinner which primarily gives the impression of middle age in the hero; but it is his whole attitude towards life, his humorous acceptance of reality as it is, and his utter incapacity for sentimental self-delusion. That is a fatal—in fact, the most fatal— defect in a lover. Love, without it, is robbed of its poetry. It becomes a sordid thing; a physical attraction, or mental compatibility; a mere prose prologue to matrimony. It is because youth constitutes nine-tenths of the public of the

American author, that the American novel (if it aims at popularity) is obliged to pander to this self-delusion, and represent life as, according to youth's sanguine scheme, it ought to be. It must blink facts, or view them in a vague and general way through romantic spectacles. The author must play Providence, and with a Rhadamantine justice reward lowly virtue and visit retribution upon prosperous wickedness. He must reconstruct the scheme of things in accordance with the ideal demands of his reader, or forfeit his popularity. Not that I blame youth for demanding a so-called poetic justice! No, I envy it. I wish I were myself capable of that charming delusion; or capable of pretending that I believed in it, even though my faith had departed.

Now I do not mean to imply that middle age, though it may have lost the highest zest in existence, is without its compensations. I admit there is a touch of exquisitely cruel regret in the thought that I am henceforth no more to be numbered among that happy throng to whom folly is becoming and permissible; that I am henceforth incapable, by my approach or departure, of accelerating the pulse of the sweet girls who are yet capable of accelerating mine; that, matrimonially speaking, I am no longer of any account (having made, once for all, a felicitous choice). No one who has passed the fatal meridian of forty will deny that there is something humiliating in the fact that (even though you were unattached) you would now cut a comic figure as a lover, and no maiden's heart would incline naturally to you, except with a filial devotion, or from sordid and worldly motives. The sweet unrest, the mysterious fascination, the fine, healthy, primeval passion, which inspire the noblest poetry of life, you are no longer capable of awakening, though you may still flatter yourself that you are capable of feeling it. You are growing stout; you are compelled to be a little prudent about your health (though you take care to disguise your caution or exercise it on the sly), and finally the first gray hair (which you scrupulously eliminate) strikes the fatal conviction to your heart that you are no longer young—that your youthful pretences are hollow and transparent shams which deceive no one but yourself. In fact, I know nothing more tragic than a man's discovery of that first gray hair; unless it be a woman's discovery of it.

But, pardon me, I forgot that it was the compensations of middle life I was to speak about, not its privations. There is a poem by Robert Browning (and a noble poem it is), which puts the case at issue between youth and age with marvellous force and insight. I shall not now quarrel with the sentiment of the opening verse, though some years ago I should have found it more than problematic:

> "Grow old along with me!
>   *The best is yet to be,*
> *The last of life for which the first was made.*
>   Our times are in His hand
>   Who saith: A whole I planned,
> Youth shows but half; trust God; see all, nor
>   be afraid."

There is something wondrously consoling in this reflection that youth is but the preparation for something better to come, a somewhat fantastically decorated vestibule through which we enter into the more soberly upholstered house where we are to dwell, and where our best and most effective work is to be done. The youth really builds the house in which he is to dwell as a man (except in the few cases in which his fathers have built it for him), and its commodiousness and beauty of style depend upon the strength and the genius that are in him. Many of us erected during our turbulent years, while we were repeating the perennial folly of the race, a very much better and handsomer and more commodious edifice than we were aware of; and we live secure in our moderate prosperity, happy in congenial labor and in the affection of our children. Though we may have to accommodate ourselves to a more prosaic jog-trot than we once thought compatible with our fiery genius, we find a deep satisfaction in the very toil and obligations which impede our speed. There are yet a hundred things which we would like to do, but which, out of regard for those who are dear to us, we have to refrain from doing.

I know a middle-aged engineer, now far past the meridian, who has been walking about for twenty years with an immortal epic in his brain, and will be walking about with it till the day when he will be confined within a narrow rosewood box from which no epic, even if ever so immortal, can escape. But I verily believe that that epic (which, on account of family necessities he never will get a chance to write) has benefited its author more than it ever would have done, if it had appeared in cold print. It has redeemed his life from the commonplace. It has given him the precious feeling of being exceptional—of being something more than the world gave him credit for being; and, finally, it has lifted his existence to a higher plane by giving him sympathy with lofty though futile endeavor.

> "Far thence—a paradox
>   Which comforts while it mocks—
> Shall life succeed in that it seems to fail?
>   What I aspired to be,
>   But was not, comforts me:
> A brute I might have been, but would not
>   sink i' the scale.

"But all the world's coarse thumb
  And finger failed to plumb,
So passed in making up the main account;
  All instincts immature,
  All purposes unsure,
That weighed not as his work, yet swelled the man's amount;

"Thoughts hardly to be packed
  Into a narrow act;
Fancies that broke through language and escaped;
  All I could never be,
  All men ignored in me—
This I was worth to God, whose wheel the pitcher shaped."

It may be a somewhat ethereal compensation which the poet here hints at, but on that account none the less real. You will contend that it lies beyond the experience of most men, and is, therefore, not typical. But I doubt if to the grossly material man, incapable of harboring such aspirations, middle age has any compensation beyond the mere satisfaction in outward prosperity and in agreeable family relations. It is the highly developed individual who points the way for the race; who by anticipating the normal development reveals what is possible to all. The highest pleasures of life are those which cannot be measured by rule of thumb; and the keenest delights are not those of achievement, but those of anticipation. Only the aspiring man is truly a man. Some mocking hope, some secret fantastic yearning—corresponding to the epic in the engineer's brain—is to be found in many more lives than we are apt to suspect. It is the spark of youth's Promethean fire astray amid the gray realities of middle age; and if you can contrive to carry this spark along with you and to keep it alive, you need have no fear of crossing the fatal meridian.

September 23, 1888

THE END

HARPER'S AMERICAN ESSAYISTS.
With Portraits. 16mo, Cloth, $1 00 each.

LITERARY AND SOCIAL SILHOUETTES. By HJALMAR HJORTH BOYESEN.

STUDIES OF THE STAGE. By BRANDER MATTHEWS.

AMERICANISMS AND BRITICISMS, with Other Essays on Other Isms By BRANDER MATTHEWS.

AS WE GO. By CHARLES DUDLEY WARNER. With Illustrations.

AS WE WERE SAYING. By CHARLES DUDLEY WARNER. With Illustrations.

FROM THE EASY CHAIR. By GEORGE WILLIAM CURTIS.

FROM THE EASY CHAIR. *Second Series.* By GEORGE WILLIAM CURTIS.

FROM THE EASY CHAIR. *Third Series.* By GEORGE WILLIAM CURTIS.

CRITICISM AND FICTION. By WILLIAM DEAN HOWELLS.

FROM THE BOOKS OF LAURENCE HUTTON.

CONCERNING ALL OF US. By THOMAS WENTWORTH HIGGINSON.

THE WORK OF JOHN RUSKIN. By CHARLES WALDSTEIN.

PICTURE AND TEXT. By HENRY JAMES. With Illustrations.

PUBLISHED BY HARPER & BROTHERS, NEW YORK.

☞ *For sale by all booksellers, or will be sent by the publishers, postage prepaid, to any part of the United States, Canada, or Mexico, on receipt of the price.*

www.ingramcontent.com/pod-product-compliance
Lightning Source LLC
Chambersburg PA
CBHW031814230426
43669CB00009B/1141